Integrated Korean

Intermediate 2

KLEAR Textbooks in Korean Language

Integrated Korean

Intermediate 2

Third Edition

Young-mee Cho Hyo Sang Lee Carol Schulz Ho-min Sohn Sung-Ock Sohn

University of Hawai'i Press
Honolulu

Printed in the United States of America
25 24 23 22 21 20 6 5 4 3 2 1

This textbook series has been developed by the Korean Language Education and Research Center (KLEAR) with the support of the Korea Foundation.

Library of Congress Cataloging-in-Publication Data
Names: Cho, Young-mee Yu, author. | Lee, Hyo Sang, author. | Schulz, Carol (Carol H.), author. | Sohn, Ho-min, author. | Sohn, Sung-Ock S., author.
Title: Integrated Korean. Intermediate / Young-mee Cho, Hyo Sang Lee, Carol Schulz, Ho-min Sohn, Sung-Ock Sohn.
Other titles: KLEAR textbooks in Korean language.
Description: Third edition. | Honolulu : University of Hawai'i Press, 2020. | Series: KLEAR textbooks in Korean language
Identifiers: LCCN 2019058802 | ISBN 9780824886776 (v. 1 ; paperback) | ISBN 9780824886820 (v. 2 ; paperback)
Subjects: LCSH: Korean language—Textbooks for foreign speakers—English.
Classification: LCC PL913 .C4843 2020 | DDC 495.782/421—dc23
LC record available at https://lccn.loc.gov/2019058802

Page design by Hyun Jun Lee
Illustrations by Seijin Han

Audio files for this volume may be downloaded in MP3 format at https://kleartextbook.com.

Printer-ready copy has been provided by KLEAR.

University of Hawai'i Press books are printed on acid-free paper and meet the guidelines for permanence and durability of the Council on Library Resources.

Contents

Preface to the Third Edition

The Integrated Korean (IK) inaugural volumes, *Beginning 1* and *Beginning 2*, of the Korean Language Education & Research Center (KLEAR) appeared in 2001. They were followed by *Intermediate, Advanced Intermediate* (now *High Intermediate*), *Advanced*, and *High Advanced* volumes. The IK series, especially the beginning and intermediate books, have attracted a large number of learners of Korean around the world, especially in the United States and other English-speaking countries. Currently, some one hundred universities and colleges use them for regular classroom instruction. The IK series is popular because the authors endeavored to develop each volume in accordance with performance-based principles and methodology: contextualization, learner-centeredness, use of authentic materials, usage-orientedness, balance between acquiring and using skills and, above all, the integration of speaking, listening, reading, writing, and culture. In addition, grammar points are systematically introduced with simple but adequate explanations and abundant examples and exercises.

Over the years, classroom teachers and students, as well as the authors themselves, noticed minor shortcomings in the first- and second-year volumes that called for improvement. Consequently, at the original authors' recommendation, a revision team was formed for the second edition consisting of Mee-Jeong Park (coordinator), Sang-Suk Oh, Joowon Suh, and Mary Shin Kim. With a strong commitment to offering the best possible learning opportunities, the team efficiently reorganized and restructured the material based on feedback received from an extensive survey. The second edition of the beginning and intermediate texts and their accompanying workbooks appeared in 2009–2013.

A few years ago a decision was made to improve and refine the intermediate volumes to anticipate the needs of today's students and instructors. The following revision team has taken on this task:

Mee-Jeong Park, University of Hawai'i at Mānoa (Coordinator)

Mary Shin Kim, University of Hawai'i at Mānoa

Joowon Suh, Columbia University

Seonkyung Jeon, University of California at Los Angeles

Several instructors of Korean at various universities in the United States, primarily University of Hawai'i alumni, have been brought on board to provide editorial support: Sooran Pak (University of Southern California), Hye Young Smith (UH Mānoa), Jason Sung (Kapi'olani Community College), and UH Mānoa doctoral students Meghan Delaney, Tyler Miyashiro, and HwanHee Kim.

The third edition of *Intermediate 1–2* differs from the second in the following respects: First, it features an attractive full-color design with new photos and illustrations; second, most of the conversations have been revised for more natural interactions within each theme-based context; third, some of the grammar points in lessons 1 through 4 have been rearranged to better reflect their level of difficulty; and fourth, the number of total lessons has been slightly reduced by removing lesson 13 and redistributing some of its grammar points to other lessons.

On behalf of KLEAR and the original authors of the intermediate volumes of Integrated Korean, I wholeheartedly thank the revision team for their tireless effort and dedication.

Ho-min Sohn
KLEAR President
July 2020

Objectives

Lesson 8 생일 파티 [Birthday Party]	
Texts	**Grammar**
Conversation 1 민지랑 마크를 초대하자.	1. The indirect question: ~지? 2. ~(으)ㄹ 테니까 'as (I) intend/expect'
Conversation 2 생일 축하해, 스티브!	3. ~느라고 'as a result of/while/because of ~ing' 4. ~(으)ㄴ/는/(으)ㄹ 줄 알다/모르다 'know/knew; don't know/didn't know'
Narration 스티브의 일기 2	
Culture	**Usage**
생일 잔치	1. Organizing a party 2. Writing invitations and thank-you notes 3. Expressing regrets

Lesson 9 미용실과 이발소 [Beauty Salons and Barbershops]	
Texts	**Grammar**
Conversation 1 자연스럽게 해 주세요.	1. 하다 versus 되다 2. ~게 하다 'make someone/something . . .'
Conversation 2 어떻게 깎아 드릴까요?	3. ~는/(으)ㄴ 거예요/거야 'The fact is . . .' 4. Causative ~이/~히/~리/~기/~우
Narration 스티브의 일기 3	
Culture	**Usage**
이발소와 미용실	1. Describing hairstyles and hair fashions 2. Commenting on someone's appearance 3. Reading and making ads

Lesson 10 취미 생활 [Hobbies]	
Texts	**Grammar**
Conversation 1 시간 있을 때 주로 뭐 하세요?	1. Expressing change in momentum: ~었/았다(가) 2. Expressing speaker's past experience: ~더라고(요).
Conversation 2 어떤 프로그램을 자주 보니?	3. ~어/아(서) 죽겠다 '. . . to death' 4. ~기도 하다 'sometimes . . . too' 5. ~어/아 버리다 'do completely'
Narration 현대인의 취미 생활	

Culture	Usage
씨름	1. Talking about stressful events 2. Talking about hobbies and pastimes 3. Reporting one's past experiences

Lesson 11 한국의 명절 [Holidays in Korea]	
Texts	**Grammar**
Conversation 1 새해 복 많이 받으세요.	1. V.S.~나 보다/A.S.~(으)ㄴ가 보다 'It seems/I guess' 2. ~기는 . . . ~다/하다 'do . . . , but'
Conversation 2 송편 먹어 본 적 있어요?	3. ~거나 'V1 or V2' 4. Expressing hearsay: ~대요/(이)래요 5. N-(이)라면 'if it were/is'
Narration 민족 대이동	
Culture	**Usage**
떡국	1. Talking about holidays 2. Making suggestions and arranging schedules 3. Reading newspaper article

Lesson 12 병원과 약국 [Hospitals and Drugstores]	
Texts	**Grammar**
Conversation 1 어디가 불편하세요?	1. A.S.~(으)ㄴ가요?/V.S.~나요? 'Is it (the case), like . . . ?' 2. Expressing regret: ~(으)ㄹ 걸 (그랬어요).
Conversation 2 문병 와 줘서 고마워.	3. ~(으)려다가 'about to but then . . .' 4. Expressing new discovery: ~군요/구나 5. Indefinite pronouns-(이)든지 'any . . .'
Narration 건강한 생활	
Culture	**Usage**
서양의학과 한의학	1. Describing illnesses and injuries 2. Describing a car accident

Lesson 13 문화 차이 [Cultural Differences]	
Texts	**Grammar**
Conversation 1 한국 문화는 알면 알수록 재미있어요.	1. ~(으)ㄴ/는데도 'despite the fact that' 2. (~(으)면) ~(으)ㄹ수록 'the more . . . the more'

Main Characters

Minji
Korean-Canadian

Soojin
Soobin's younger sister
Senior in high school

Hyunwoo
Good at cooking

Yujin
Likes working out and going to baseball games

8과 생일 파티

Lesson 8 Birthday Party

Conversation 1 민지랑 마크를 초대하자.

현우와 유진이가 만나서 이야기한다.

Conversation 1

현우: 다음 주 금요일이 스티브 생일이라던데.

유진: 아, 맞아. 깜빡 잊어버렸네.
우리 스티브 생일 파티 해 줄까?

현우: 그래, 그러자. 근데 어디서 하지?G8.1

유진: 지난 번에 보니까 수빈이 아파트가 넓던데.

현우: 그래. 내가 한번 물어볼게.

유진: 누구를 초대하지?

현우: 민지랑 마크를 초대하자. 스티브하고 친하잖아.

유진: 그럼 모두 여섯 명이네.

현우: 저녁 준비는 수빈이하고 내가 할 테니까G8.2
너는 다른 사람들한테 연락해 줄래?

유진: 그래. 내가 문자 보낼게.
몇 시까지 모이라고 할까?

현우: 여섯 시쯤 모이지 뭐.

유진: 그래, 그게 좋겠다.

COMPREHENSION QUESTIONS

1. 스티브 생일이 언제입니까?
2. 생일 파티를 어디서 하려고 합니까?
3. 생일 파티에 누구를 초대하려고 합니까?
4. 누가 무엇을 준비하기로 했습니까?

NEW WORDS

NOUN

김밥	*kimbap*
낮잠	nap
동영상	video, movie file
떡볶이	spicy rice cake
문자	text message
아무거나	anything
재료	ingredient, material
초	candle
초대(하다)	invitation
초대장	invitation card
초콜릿	chocolate
카메라	camera
케이크	cake
팀	team
회의	meeting

POSTNOUN

(이)네	[person]'s place

VERB

끝내다	to end
모이다	to gather
올리다	to post up, upload
잊어버리다	to forget

ADJECTIVE

급하다	be urgent
정신없다	be mindless
친하다	be close to someone

ADVERB

깜빡	with a flash
여태	still, so far yet

COUNTER

호	number, issue

SUFFIX

~(으)ㄹ 테니까	as (I) intend . . .
~던데	though, in spite of
~지?	indirect question

NEW EXPRESSIONS

1. 금요일이 스티브 생일이라던데.

~던데 (from 더 + (으)ㄴ데) in the above sentence expresses some background circumstance experienced earlier that contrasts with the current situation.

2. 잊어버리다: When the verb 버리다 'to throw away' is used after V.S.~어/아, it has an idiomatic usage expressing the finality or completion of an action.

잊어버리다	'to forget completely'
먹어 버리다	'to eat everything'

3. 초대 'invitation', 초대장 'a (written) invitation', 초대하다 'to invite'

Grammar

G8.1 The indirect question: ~지?

Examples

(1) A: 한국어 인터뷰 준비하는데 뭘 공부해야 되**지**?
B: 단어를 많이 알아야 될 거야. 주말에 같이 공부할래?
A: 어, 그래. 같이 하자.

(2) A: 스티브 생일이 언제**지**?
B: 다음주 토요일이잖아.
A: 우리 스티브 생일 파티 해 줄까?
B: 그래, 그러자. 근데 어디서 하**지**?
A: 수빈이네 아파트가 넓으니까 수빈이네 아파트에서 하자.

(3) A: 왜 이렇게 배가 아프**지**?
B: 너 아까 점심 먹고 바로 낮잠 잤잖아.
약 좀 사 먹어.
A: 그래, 그래야겠다.

Notes

1. ~지(요) can be used in an information question with a question word (누(구), 뭐, 어디, 언제, or 어떻게). The information question with ~지 is not a question plainly seeking information, but it is as if the speaker ought to know the answer but somehow the information is missing, and thus wonders about the information asked.

2. The information question with ~지 sounds like the speaker is consulting the listener in seeking information.

3. The question with ~지(요) is less imposing on the listener, because the speaker is not directly asking the listener to provide an answer, but helping the speaker retrieve the missing information; that is, the listener does not get to feel obliged to provide an answer. Therefore, the information question with ~지 is more polite than a plain information question.

Exercises

1. Based on the given answers, reconstruct information questions indicating that the speaker is wondering about information that is sought and asking the listener to help him/her retrieve the missing information.

(1) A: ______________________________

B: 오늘 회의는 이스트 홀 301호에서 해요.

(2) A: ______________________________

B: 청소하러 마크가 올 거예요.

(3) A: ______________________________

B: 제 생일은 오월 이십구일이에요.

(4) A: ______________________________

B: 한국의 수도는 서울이에요.

2. Reconstruct a dialogue that occurs in the given situations below. Speaker A is seeking information that speaker B might have.

(1) A mutual friend, Steve's birthday is coming up, but speaker A does not remember exactly when Steve's birthday is.

A: ______________________________?

B: ______________________________.

(2) A is looking for a post office in the area.

A: ______________________________?

B: ______________________________.

(3) A met B some time ago and does not remember his/her name.

A: ______________________________?

B: ______________________________.

(4) A and B are expecting an important guest, and are not sure what food and drink to serve.

A: ______________________________?

B: ______________________________.

(5) A and B are asked to sing at a party, but A does not know what to sing.

A: ______________________________?

B: ______________________________.

Notes

G8.2 ~(으)ㄹ 테니까 'as (I) intend/expect'

Examples

(1) 유진: 생일 파티에 난 뭐 준비할까?
동수: 케이크랑 초는 내가 준비 **할 테니까** 너는 초대장 좀 보내 줄래?
Because I will get the cake and the candles, would you like to mail the invitations?

(2) [소연 is notorious for being late.]
동수: 소연 씨가 아직 안 왔는데 조금만 더 기다릴까요?
마크: 소연 씨는 또 늦게 **늦을 테니까** 우리 먼저 가요.
Since 소연 will be late again, let's go ahead.

(3) [소연 calls while everybody else is waiting for dinner.]
성희: 왜 여태 안 와?
소연: 응. 나 15분 후에 **갈 테니까** 기다리지 말고 먼저 먹어.

(4) [B has just come back from a conference abroad.]
A: 그동안 한국 음식 못 **먹었을 테니까** 내가 떡볶이 사 줄게.
B: 아니야. 호텔 앞에 한국 식당이 있어서 매일 사 먹었어. 그냥 아무거나 먹어도 돼.

Notes

1. Recall that ~(으)니까 provides reasons or grounds to justify what the speaker says subsequently. ~(으)ㄹ 테니까 provides the speaker's assumed reasons or intentions.

2. ~(으)ㄹ 테니까 is a contracted form of ~(으)ㄹ 터이니까, which literally means 'Since the situation would be . . .' Note that ~(으)ㄹ is a prospective noun-modifying form. The original meaning of 터 is a 'place' or 'site', but here it is used in a more abstract sense to refer to intention or assumption. 이 'to be' is a copula.

Exercises

Using ~(으)ㄹ 테니까, make up an utterance that is appropriate for the given context.

(1) [여행사에서]

샌디: 요즘 뉴욕까지 왕복 얼마예요?

직원: 요즘은 좀 비싸요. $950이에요.

_______________________ 그 때 사세요.

샌디: 12월1일부터 세일이에요?

직원: 네, 아마 $100정도 싸질 거예요.

(2) 동수: 소연아, 왜 빨리 안 와. 급한데 우리 먼저 갈까?

소연: 어, 정신없이 일하다가 깜빡 잊어버렸어.

_______________________ 조금만 기다려 줘.

동수: 5시 30분까지 올래? 그럼 그때까지 기다릴게.

(3) 유진: 우리 김밥 만들어 먹을까?

동수: 그래. 그럼 내가 재료를 _______________________

너는 밥 좀 할래?

유진: 좋아. 한국마켓에 가 봐. 요즘 세일하더라.

(4) 민지: 우리 팀 프로젝트 내일까지 다 끝내야 되는데

인터넷에서 사진을 아직 못 찾았어.

소연: 그럼 사진은 내가 _______________________

넌 유튜브에서 동영상 좀 찾아 줄래?

민지: 그래, 그럴게.

CULTURE

생일 잔치 Birthday Party

한국에서는 아기가 태어난 지 100일째 되는 날에 떡과 술, 음식을 장만하여[1] '백일' 잔치를 연다. 떡은 이웃들과 함께 나누어[2] 먹는데, 100명의 이웃[3]이 떡을 나누어 먹으면 아기가 100살까지 살 수 있다고 믿어 왔다. 이웃들은 떡을 먹은 후 빈 접시[4]에 장수[5]를 기원하는[6] 의미의 실이나 미래의 부[7]를 상징하는[8] 쌀이나 돈을 담아[9] 돌려 준다.

한국인에게 인생에서 가장 큰 두 번의 생일은 첫 번째 생일인 '돌'과 60번째 생일인 '환갑' 혹은 '회갑'이다. 이 두 번의 생일은 친척들과 이웃들을 초대해 큰 잔치를 연다. 오래되고 드물다[10]는 뜻으로 '고희' 혹은 '칠순'이라고 불리는[11] 70번째 생일은 보통 가족들과 잔치를 하는 편이다.

돌, 환갑, 고희만큼은 아니지만 다른 생일에도 가족들과 함께 음식을 나누며 축하를 한다.

1. 장만하다: to purchase, prepare
2. 나누다: to share
3. 이웃: neighbor
4. 접시: plate
5. 장수: long life
6. 기원하다: to wish
7. 미래의 부: future wealth
8. 상징하다: to symbolize
9. 담다: to put something into something
10. 드물다: be rare
11. 불리다: be called

Conversation 2 생일 축하해, 스티브!

수빈이 아파트에 마크와 유진이가 와서 초인종을 누른다.

Conversation 2

수빈: 누구세요?

유진: 수빈아, 우리 왔어.

수빈: (문을 열면서)
어서 와. 준비할 게 많은데 일찍 와서
다행이다. 근데 민지는 같이 안 왔어?

유진: 어, 빵집에서 디저트 사 가지고 금방 올 거야.

마크: 와, 맛있는 냄새 난다.

수빈: 응, 현우가 지금 부엌에서 미역국 끓이고 있어.

수빈이 아파트에 마크와 유진이가 와서 초인종을 누른다.

수빈: 스티브, 어서 들어 와.

모두: 생일 축하해, 스티브!

스티브: 고마워. 음식 준비하느라고[G8.3] 고생 많았겠다.

수빈: 아니야, 모두 도와 줘서 금방 끝났어.

부엌에서

스티브: 이 국은 무슨 국이야? 처음 보는데.

현우: 미역국이야. 한국 사람들은 생일날 꼭 미역국을 먹거든. 먹어 봐.

스티브: 맛있다. 요리를 이렇게 잘 하는 줄 몰랐어.[G8.4]

COMPREHENSION QUESTIONS

1. 유진은 왜 민지와 같이 오지 않았습니까?
2. 현우는 부엌에서 무엇을 하고 있습니까?
3. 스티브가 처음 먹어 본 음식은 무엇입니까?

NEW WORDS

NOUN

국	soup
냄새	smell
농담	joke
디저트	dessert
마트	discount stores
모임	gathering
미역국	seaweed soup
샴페인	champagne
소원	wish
솜씨	skill, ability
초인종	doorbell
촛불	candlelight
통화(하다)	phone call

ADJECTIVE

다행이다	be fortunate, relieved

VERB

끄다	to turn off
끓이다	to boil
냄새 나다	to smell
누르다	to press, push
내다	to turn in
마치다	to finish
빌다	to beg; ask for

ADVERB

꼭	surely, certainly
얼마	some (time, amount)
이렇게	like this, this way
전혀	not at all

SUFFIX

~느라고	because of ~ing
~는/(으)ㄴ 줄 알다/모르다	know/don't know know/knew; don't know/didn't know

NEW EXPRESSIONS

1. When 어서 'quickly' is used in the following expressions, it is not pushy but instead has a sense of welcoming.

어서 들어와.	Come right in.
어서 와.	Come in (welcome).

Grammar

G8.3 ~느라고 'as a result of/while/because of ~ing'

Examples

(1) A: 어디 가세요?
B: 동호회 모임에 가는 길이에요.
여름에 한국 갔다 오**느라고** 한 번도 못 갔거든요.

(2) A: 어제 수진 씨랑 통화했어요?
B: 아뇨. 어제 숙제 마치**느라고** 시간이 전혀 없었어요.

(3) A: 떡볶이 먹**느라** 샴페인을 잊어버렸네요.
B: 아, 제가 가져 올게요.

(4) A: 얼른 케이크 촛불 꺼야지요.
B: 아, 소원 비**느라고**요.

Notes

1. ~느라고 'as a result of doing . . . , while doing . . . , because of ~ing' indicates that one is engaged in one action or event at the expense of another.

2. Note that ~느라고 is typically followed by an expression of negative implication, to indicate that the person fails to carry out the action that is called for, as in examples (1)–(3). ~느라고 cannot occur with a main clause in the form of request or command. The suffix 고 of 느라고 can be omitted as in example (3) and still convey the same meaning.

3. ~느라고 is used only with verbs, and no tense marking suffix can be added to ~느라고. The main clause may be omitted in casual conversation as in example (4).

Exercises

Using ~느라고, answer the following questions.

(1) 유진: 어제 텔레비전에서 야구 경기 봤어요?
수연: 아니요. 숙제하느라고 못 봤어요.

(2) A: 어제 잠을 못 잤어요?
B: ______________________.

(3) 선생님: 지난 생일에 미역국 먹었어요?
학생: ______________________.

(4) A: 요즘 어떻게 지내세요?
B: ______________________.

(5) A: 어제 스티브 생일 파티에 왜 안 왔어요?
B: ______________________.

(6) A: 요새 왜 테니스 치러 안 나오세요?
B: ______________________.

Notes

G8.4 ~(으)ㄴ/는/(으)ㄹ 줄 알다/모르다 'know/knew; don't know/didn't know'

Examples

(1) 동수: 제가 만든 된장찌개예요.
맛있게 드세요.
민지: 와, 맛있다! 동수 씨가 이렇게 요리 솜씨가 좋**은 줄** 정말 **몰랐어요**.
Wow, it's delicious! I really didn't know your cooking ability was this good.

(2) 마크: 성희 씨, 불고기 더 없어요?
성희: 어머, 어떡하죠?
불고기 다 먹었는데. 이렇게 많이 먹**을 줄 몰랐어요**.
I didn't think we would eat this much.
2kg이면 **될 줄 알았는데**.
I thought two kilograms would be enough.

(3) 성희: 아니, 유진 씨, 초가 왜 스물 두 개밖에 없어요?
유진: 스티브 스물두 살 아니에요?
성희: 아이, 스물세 살이잖아요.
마크: 유진 씨는 스티브가 스물두 살**인 줄 알아요**.
유진: 네. 저는 스물두 살**인 줄 알았어요**.

Notes

1. ~는/(으)ㄴ/(으)ㄹ 줄 알다/모르다 is used to express a presumed thought. That is, ~는/(으)ㄴ/(으)ㄹ 줄 알다 refers to what the subject thinks or thought would happen. ~는/(은)ㄴ/(으)ㄹ 줄 모르다 refers to a thought which the subject fails to come up with.

2. The presumed thought marked by ~는/(으)ㄴ/(으)ㄹ 줄 알다 may or may not turn out to be true. If it does, ~는/(으)ㄴ/(으)ㄹ 줄 알다 can be translated as '. . . know/knew ~'. If it does not, it can be translated as '. . . think/thought ~'.

3. The variation among ~는 줄 알다, ~(으)ㄴ 줄 알다, and ~(으)ㄹ 줄 알다 has to do with the time of the situation described:

~는 줄 알다:	The time of the situation described is the same as when the subject has the thought of it.
~(으)ㄴ 줄 알다:	The time of the situation described is prior to the time when the subject has the thought of it. [Note that adjectives and the copula ~이 take ~(으)ㄴ/~(이)ㄴ 줄 알다 regardless of the time of thought.
~(으)ㄹ 줄 알다:	The subject's thought is about what would happen.

Exercises

Make up an utterance that is appropriate for the given context.

(1) A: 숙제 다 했어요?
B: 어, 내일까지 내는 거 아니에요?
<u>내일까지 해 오는 건 줄 알았어요</u>.

(2) 유진: 동수 있어요?
동수 누나: 네, 근데 지금 자는 것 같은데요.
동수: 누나! 나 아직 안 자.
동수 누나: 아, 아직 안 자네요.
________________________________.

(3) A: 저 앞에 있는 여자 머리 예쁘지요?
B: 네, 머리가 정말 긴데요.
A: 농담이에요. 저 사람 제 남자 친구예요.
B: 아, 머리가 길어서 ________________________.

(4) A: 퀴즈 공부 많이 했어요?
B: 네? 오늘 퀴즈 있어요? ________________________.

Narration 생일 잔치

한국에 온 지 6개월이 되었다. 그동안 정신없이 바빠서 생일인 것도 잊어버리고 있었다. 그런데 한국에서 사귄 친구들이 오늘 생일 파티를 해 주었다. 한국에서는 생일 날에 미역국을 먹는다고 한다. 미역국을 처음 먹어 봤는데 아주 맛있었다. 수빈이가 만든 떡볶이와 김밥도 정말 맛있었다. 내가 초콜릿을 좋아하는 걸 알고 민지가 초콜릿 케이크를 사 왔다. 그런데 내가 스물한 살이 되는 줄 모르고 초를 스무 개만 가져 왔다. 친구들이 생일 축하 노래를 불러 주었다. 그리고, 나는 한국에서 친구들과 계속 잘 지냈으면 좋겠다고 소원을 빌면서 촛불을 껐다.

COMPREHENSION QUESTIONS

1. 스티브는 생일 파티 때 어떤 음식을 먹었습니까?
2. 민지는 무엇을 사 왔습니까?
3. 스티브는 몇 살이 되었습니까?
4. 스티브는 어떤 소원을 빌었습니까?

NEW EXPRESSIONS

1. 정신없이: 정신 means 'mind, mental state', and the commonly used expression 정신없다 means 'be mindless, to have no time even to think'.

Notes

USAGE

1 *Organizing a party*

동수 organizes a birthday party for 유진. The following is 동수's memo for the party.

장소:	동수 아파트
날짜:	1월 5일 금요일 6시
초대할 사람들:	성희, 마크, 민지, 스티브, 소연
음식:	불고기, 미역국, 잡채, 밥, 김치
	(음식은 동수와 성희가 같이 준비함)
생일 케이크:	소연이가 준비함
음료수:	스티브가 준비함
선물:	친구들이 각자 하나씩 준비

Exercise 1

Based on 동수's memo, ask your partner the following questions:

(1) 생일 파티에 몇 사람을 초대하기로 했습니까?

(2) 생일날 음식은 누가 만들기로 했습니까?

(3) 마실 것은 누가 준비하기로 했습니까?

(4) 생일 선물은 어떻게 하기로 했습니까?

Exercise 2

You plan to host a party for your friend who is going to graduate next Sunday. Make a list of things to do to organize the party, and present your list to the class.

Exercise 3

Converse with your partner on the following topics:

(1) 가장 재미있었던 생일 파티

(2) 가장 기억에 남는 생일 선물 (기억에 남는 memorable)

(3) 다음 생일날 받고 싶은 선물

(4) 제일 친한 친구의 생일날 주고 싶은 선물

Exercise 4

Role play

(1) You are organizing a surprise party for your friend's birthday. There are many things to be done. Call and ask each of your friends to do something for the party.

(2) You talk with a Korean student about birthday customs in Korea. Ask how Korean people celebrate birthdays, what kinds of presents are usually given, and what kinds of food are served on the birthday.

2 *Writing invitations and thank-you notes*

동수 wrote invitations for 유진's birthday party.

여러분을 한유진의 스물두 번째 생일에 초대합니다.

꼭 오셔서 축하해 주십시오.

· 시간: 1월 5일 금요일 저녁 6시

· 장소: 김동수네 집

영등포구 여의도동 상호 아파트 3동 607호

· 전화 번호: 780-6331

Writing thank-you notes

유진 wrote a thank-you note to 동수 for hosting his birthday party.

> 동수 씨,
> 생일 파티를 해 주셔서 정말 감사합니다. 동수 씨 덕분에 정말 즐거운 생일을 보냈습니다. 주신 생일 선물도 정말 고맙습니다. 제가 제일 좋아하는 한국 가수의 CD를 받게 되어서 무척 기뻤습니다.
>
> 2021년 2월 18일
> 유진 드림

Exercise 1

Imagine that you are planning a party for your friend's 20th birthday next Saturday at your place. Write invitations for the party.

Exercise 2

Write a thank-you note for the following situations.

(1) You received a nice watch from your Korean friend for your birthday.
(2) You came back from a dinner hosted by a Korean family. The food was delicious.
(3) Your Korean teacher wrote a letter of recommendation (추천서) for your job application.
(4) You are staying with a Korean family while studying in Seoul for a year. Your host family threw a surprise birthday party for you.

3 *Expressing regrets*

Practice the following dialogues.

(1) 민지: 김 선생님, 다음 주 토요일에 마크 씨 생일 파티가 있는데 오실 수 있으세요?
김 선생님: 어떡하죠? 다음 주말에 일본에 있는 친구가 오는데.
민지: 그러세요? 파티에 꼭 오시면 좋겠네요.

(2) 성희: 민지 씨, 김 선생님이 아직 파티에 안 오셨네요.
민지: 오늘 못 오신다고 하셨어요. <u>일본에서 친구분이 오신대요</u>.
성희: 그래요? 오실 줄 알았는데 섭섭하네요.

Exercise 1

Substitute the underlined parts above for the following and practice the conversation with your classmate.

(1) Prof. Kim has a severe headache.
(2) Prof. Kim has an important appointment.
(3) Prof. Kim's parents visit him from Seoul.
(4) Prof. Kim has a cold.
(5) Prof. Kim's car has been broken.

Exercise 2

Role play

(1) You are invited by your Korean friend for New Year's Day celebration at his/her parents' house. You have accepted the invitation, but on New Year's Day, you have a severe headache. Call your friend and explain why you are unable to attend the party.

(2) You have made an appointment with your Korean professor. On your way to school, you witnessed a traffic accident and reported the accident to the police. You missed the appointment with your teacher. Call your teacher and explain the situation.

Lesson 8 Birthday Party

CONVERSATION 1 *Let's Invite Minji and Mark.*

Hyunwoo and Yujin meet and have a conversation

Hyunwoo: I heard next Friday is Steve's birthday.
Yujin: Oh, right. I completely forgot. Shall we throw him a birthday party?
Hyunwoo: Yeah, let's do that. But where should we have it?
Yujin: I think Soobin's apartment is pretty big.
Hyunwoo: Okay. I will ask her.
Yujin: Whom should we invite?
Hyunwoo: Let's invite Minji and Mark. They are good friends with Steve, you know.
Yujin: Then it's six people altogether.
Hyunwoo: Soobin and I will prepare the dinner, so can you contact the others?
Yujin: Okay. I'll text them. What time should I tell them to be there?
Hyunwoo: Let's gather around six, I guess.
Yujin: Okay, that sounds good.

CONVERSATION 2 *Happy Birthday, Steve!*

Mark and Yujin arrived at Soobin's apartment and rang the doorbell.

Soobin: Who is it?
Yujin: Soobin, it's us.
Soobin: (Opening the door)
Please come in. There's a lot to prepare, so I'm glad you two came early. Minji didn't come with you?
Yujin: Nope, she went to the bakery to get the dessert, so she'll be here soon.
Mark: Wow, something smells really good.
Soobin: Yeah, Hyunwoo is cooking seaweed soup in the kitchen now.
(A little later, Steve arrives at Soobin's apartment.)
Soobin: Steve, please come in.

All: Happy birthday, Steve!
Steve: Thank you. You must have worked hard to prepare the food.
Soobin: No, everyone helped, so we finished early.
Steve: What kind of soup is this? I've never seen it before.
Mark: It's seaweed soup. Koreans always eat seaweed soup on their birthdays. Try some.
Steve: It's delicious. I never knew Hyunwoo was so good at cooking.

NARRATION *Steve's Diary 2*

It's been six months since I came to Korea. I've been so busy and out of it, I forgot that it was even my birthday. But my friends I made in Korea threw me a birthday party today. They told me people eat seaweed soup on their birthday in Korea. I tried seaweed soup for the first time, and it was very delicious. The tteokbokki and gimbap that Soobin made were also really good. Minji brought a chocolate cake, because she knows that I like chocolate. But she only brought 20 candles, not knowing I am turning 21. My friends sang Happy Birthday to me. And I blew out the candles, wishing that I could continue staying in Korea with my friends.

CULTURE *Birthday Party*

In Korea, on the 100th day after a child has been born, food, alcohol, and tteok are prepared for a "100 day" party. The tteok is shared and eaten together with the neighbors; it's believed that if tteok is shared with 100 neighbors, the child will be able to live to 100 years old. After eating the tteok, the neighbors will place either a wish for longevity in the form of a string, or something that symbolizes future wealth, such as rice grains or money in the empty dish and return it.

To Koreans, the two biggest birthdays are the first birthday, called "dol," and 60th birthday, called "hwangap" or "hwegap." On these two birthdays, a huge feast is held that relatives and neighbors are invited to. On the 70th birthday, called "gohui" or "chilsun" meaning "old and uncommon," people normally tend to have a banquet with their family.

Other birthdays also are usually celebrated by eating with family, although not as extravagantly as the 1st, 60th, or 70th birthdays.

Elegance Salon

9과 미용실과 이발소

Lesson 9 Beauty Salons and Barbershops

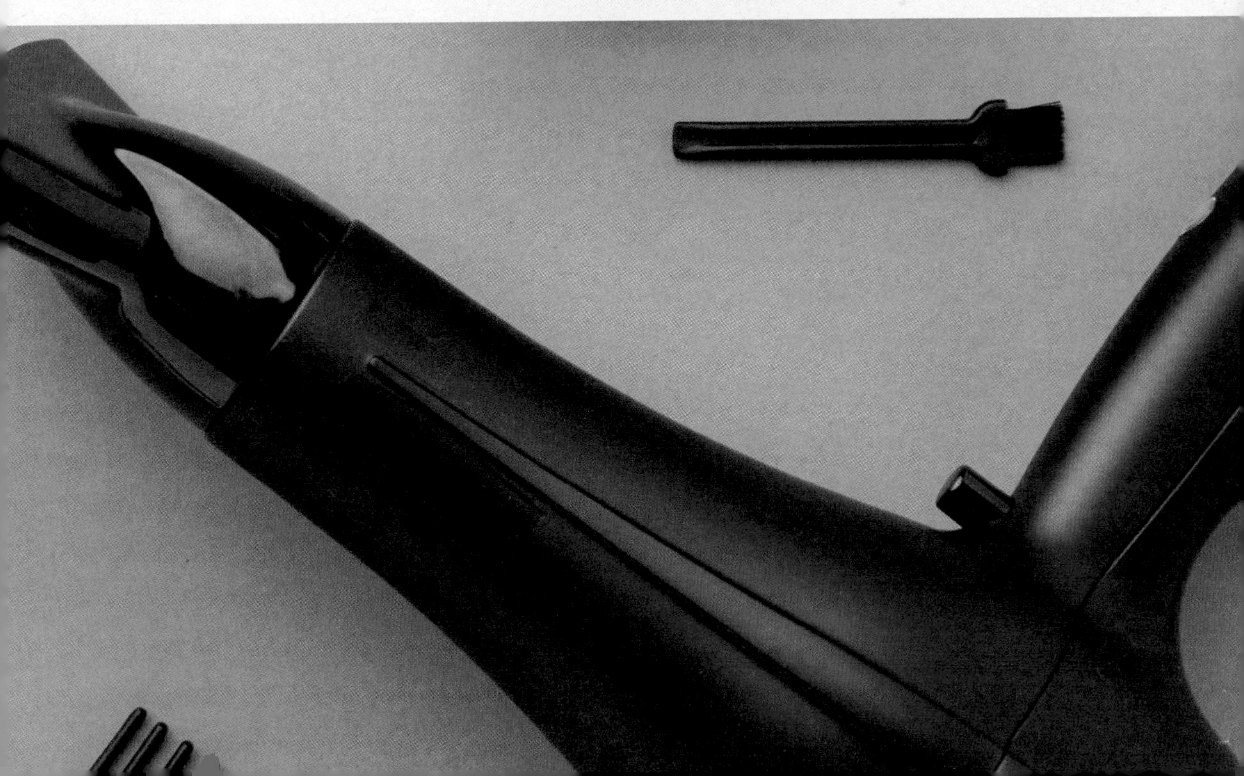

Conversation 1 자연스럽게 해 주세요.

민지는 파마를 하러 미용실에 갔다

Conversation 1

직원: 어서 오세요. 예약하셨어요?
민지: 네, 3시에 예약했는데요.
직원: 아, 김민지 님, 여기 3시로 예약되어[G9.1] 있네요. 이쪽으로 앉으세요.

잠시 후

미용사: 어떻게 해 드릴까요?
민지: 파마를 하려고 하는데요.
미용사: 어떤 스타일을 원하세요?
민지: 굵은 롤로 자연스럽게 해[G9.2] 주세요.
미용사: 머리는 얼마나 자를까요?
민지: 앞머리만 조금 잘라 주세요.
미용사: 뒷머리도 조금 다듬을까요?
민지: 네, 그렇게 해 주세요.

두 시간 후 파마가 끝났다.

미용사: 어떠세요? 마음에 드세요?
민지: 네, 예쁘네요. 그런데 이 머리 어떻게 손질해야 되지요?
미용사: 샴푸하고 나서 드라이어로 살짝 말려 주시기만 하면 돼요.
민지: 네, 알겠습니다. 감사합니다.

COMPREHENSION QUESTIONS

1. 민지는 왜 미용실에 갔습니까?
2. 민지는 어떤 스타일을 원합니까?
3. 민지는 머리를 얼마나 잘랐습니까?
4. 미용사가 머리 손질을 어떻게 하라고 했습니까?

NEW WORDS

NOUN

녹음(하다)	recording
뒷머리	hair on the back of your head
드라이어	hair dryer
롤	roll
무스	mousse
미용사	hairstylist
미용실	beauty salon
샴푸	shampoo
스타일	style
앞머리	bangs
예약(하다)	reservation, appointment
이발소	barbershop
취직(하다)	getting a job
파마(하다)	perm
화장(하다)	makeup

NOUN SUFFIX

님	honorific noun suffix

VERB

다듬다	to trim
떠들다	to make noise
말리다	to dry
(무스를) 바르다	to apply
상하다	to get damaged
손질하다	to fix up
자르다	to cut

ADJECTIVE

굵다	be thick
자연스럽다	be natural

ADVERB

살짝	slightly
잠시	briefly
앞으로	in the future

SUFFIX

~게 하다	to make someone/something . . .

NEW EXPRESSIONS

1. 다듬다 'to trim, clean'

머리를 다듬다
야채를 다듬다

2. 말리다 is a causative (transitive) verb of 마르다 'to be dry'.

머리가 잘 마르네요.
머리가 안 말라서 드라이로 말렸어요.
머리가 마를 때까지 기다릴 수가 없어요.

3. 손질 is a compound word consisting of 손 'a hand' and 질 'an act'.

도둑질	'stealing'
다림질	'ironing'
젓가락질	'using chopsticks'

4. 미용실 and 미장원 are interchangeable, although 미장원 is used more colloquially and 미용실 is used more in written form.

Grammar

G9.1 하다 versus 되다

Examples

(1) 민지: 마크 씨, 한국 갈 준비 다 **했어요**?
마크: 네, 다른 건 다 준비**됐고** 이제 비자만 받으면 돼요.

(2) 직원: 어서 오세요.
유미: 네. 토요일 3시에 예약**했는데요**.
직원: 아, 네. 김유미 님, 3시에 예약**돼** 있으시네요.

(3) 동수: 내일 시험이 어렵게 나올 것 같아서 걱정**돼요**.
성희: 동수 씨는 공부 많이 했으니까 걱정**하지** 마세요.

(4) A: 빨리 취직**해야** 되는데 쉽지가 않네요.
B: 성적이 좋으니까 곧 취직**될** 거예요.

Notes

1. Recall that both ~게 되다 and ~게 하다 involve a change of situation. The difference between the two, as indicated by their main verbs 되다 and 하다, is that with ~게 되다, the subject (a person or an object) passively undergoes the change, whereas with ~게 하다, the subject enforces the change.

The similar contrast is made with some verbs such as 예약하다/예약되다, 준비하다/준비되다, 걱정하다/걱정되다, 녹음하다/녹음되다, 취직하다/취직되다, etc. 하다 verbs express an active and volitional action on the part of the subject person, whereas 되다 verbs express that an action is acted upon the subject person and thus the subject person simply undergoes the situation passively. In (4), for example, A uses 취직하다 to indicate that A himself has been actively looking for a job and found one. B, on the other hand, uses 취직되다 to emphasize the result/outcome of the job search.

2. With 되다, the subject is typically an object or thing, rather than a person, as in (1). In this case, the focus is given to the situation or circumstance rather than an action taken by the person in question.

Exercises

Fill in the blank with an appropriate verb, using either 되다 or 하다, that would fit in the context.

(1) A: 지난 번에 내가 말한 음악 녹음했어요?
B: 아니요, 배터리가 없어서 녹음이 안 됐어요.

(2) A: 저녁 때 학교 앞 갈비집에 갈까요?
B: 거기는 미리 예약해야 되는데요.
A: 제가 아까 전화로 ______________.

(3) A: 화장 예쁘게 잘 됐네요.
B: 파티가 있어서 미용실 언니가 화장 ______ 줬어요.

(4) 민지: 마크 씨, 내일 취직시험 보러 가지요?
____________________ (are you worried)?
마크: 네, 시험이 어려울 거라고 그래서 조금
_____________네요.
민지: 너무 _____________ 마세요. (Don't worry . . .)
잘 할 거예요. 이번에 취직하면 뭐 하고 싶어요?
마크: 이번에 ______________면 차를 살 거예요.
지금 쓰는 차가 오래됐거든요.

G9.2 ~게 하다 'make someone/something . . .'

Examples

(1) 미용사: 머리 어떻게 해 드릴까요?
민지: 뒷머리는 짧게 자르고요, 앞머리는 자연스럽**게 해** 주세요.

(2) 무엇이 부모님을 가장 기쁘**게 해** 드리는 일일까요? What would please your parents most?

(3) [Notice in a construction area]
여기는 위험하니까 아이들이 들어오지 못하**게 해** 주세요! Because it's dangerous here, please do not let children come in.

(4) 어머니: (Coming back home from work)
아이들이 다 어디 있죠?
Babysitter: 이층에 있어요. 너무 떠들어서 방에서 비디오 보**게 했**어요.

(5) 머리 상하지 않**게** 조심하세요. Be careful so as not to damage your hair.

Notes

1. Recall that ~게 되다 indicates a change of situation; that is, an entity comes to be in a new situation. The change is made not by the person's volitional will, but by some external circumstance. ~게 하다 'to make/have someone/something~', on the other hand, indicates that someone willfully changes the situation so as to put an entity (a person or an object) in a new situation, that is, to have someone/something put in a new state of affairs, as in (1) and (2), or to make/have someone engage in an action, as in (3) and (4).

2. ~게 **. . .** can be used to express that an action is taken so that it would result in some situation. In this case, the construction ~게 하다 can best be translated as '. . . so that/as to ~', as in (5).

Exercises

Make up a request that is appropriate for the given context.

(1) [You want to have your hair look natural.]
(To hairdresser) 자연스럽게 해 주세요.

(2) [The children screamed loudly.]
(To the parents) ______________________________

(3) [You don't want the wall painted too dark.]
(To the painter) ______________________________

(4) [You don't want to have your makeup too heavy.]
(To the makeup artist) ______________________________

(5) [You don't want your child to watch too much TV while you are out.]
(To the babysitter) ______________________________

(6) [You don't like the room temperature too cold.]
(To the person who sets the air-conditioner)

____

Notes

Conversation 2 어떻게 깎아 드릴까요?

스티브가 머리를 깎으러 이발소에 갔다.

Conversation 2

이발사: 어떻게 깎아 드릴까요?

스티브: 단정하게 깎아 주세요.

이발사: 머리가 많이 기네요. 이발한 지 얼마나 됐어요?

스티브: 세 달쯤 된 것 같아요.

이발사: 3개월이나 머리를 안 깎으셨어요?

스티브: 제가 머리 깎는 걸 아주 귀찮아하거든요.
한국 와서 처음으로 머리를 깎는 거예요.[G9.3]

이발사: 아, 그러세요?

잠시 후에

이발사: 옆머리 어때요? 좀 더 짧게 해 드릴까요?

스티브: 네, 앞머리도 조금 더 쳐 주세요.
약간 긴 것 같아요.

이발사: 네, 알겠습니다.

잠시 후에

이발사: 저쪽으로 가서
머리 감겨[G9.4] 드릴게요.

머리 감고 나서

이발사: 마음에 드세요?

스티브: 네, 시원해 보이네요.
고맙습니다.

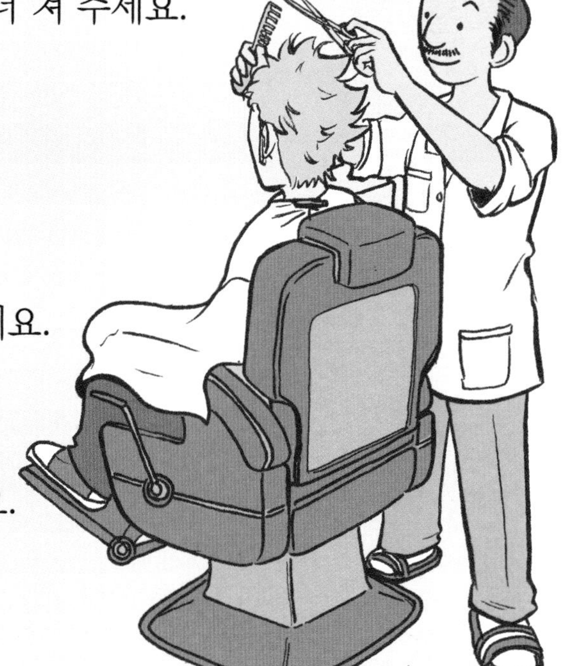

COMPREHENSION QUESTIONS

1. 스티브는 얼마 만에 이발소에 갔습니까?
2. 스티브는 왜 이발소에 자주 안 갑니까?
3. 스티브는 어떤 스타일을 원합니까?
4. 머리를 자르니까 어떻게 보입니까?

NEW WORDS

NOUN

면도(하다)	shaving
벌레	insect
아기	baby
옆머리	the side of the head
이발(하다)	haircut (for men)
이발사	barber
전문	one's specialty
팁	tip

ADJECTIVE

귀찮다	be troublesome

ADVERB

겨우	barely
당연히	of course, naturally
약간	slightly

SUFFIX

~는 거예요	the fact is . . .

VERB

감다	to wash (hair)
감기다	to wash someone's hair
깎다	to cut (hair)
깨다	to wake up
깨우다	to wake someone up
먹이다	to feed
벗기다	to take someone's clothes off
타다	to ride; burn
태우다	to give someone a ride; burn
신기다	to put (footwear) on someone
울리다	to make someone cry
웃기다	to make someone laugh
입히다	to dress someone
재우다	to get someone to sleep

NEW EXPRESSIONS

1. 머리를 깎다 'to get a haircut' (usually for men)
   머리를 자르다 'to get a haircut' (usually for women)
   앞머리를 치다 'to trim one's bangs'

2. 조금 and 약간 are mostly interchangeable, though 약간 is slightly more formal due to its origin as a Chinese borrowing. 조금 is often abbreviated as 좀.

3. 귀찮아하다 is a transitive counterpart of 귀찮다. Like the pair 좋다 and 좋아하다, 귀찮다 can take only a first-person subject in statements and a second-person subject in questions, whereas 귀찮아하다 does not have this restriction.

(나는) 머리 깎는 것이 귀찮아서 두 달에 한 번 정도 이발소에 가요.
형이 동생을 귀찮아해서 동생과 놀아 주지 않아요.

Grammar

G9.3 ~는/(으)ㄴ 거예요/거야 'The fact is . . .'

Examples

(1) 성희: 어, 얼굴을 다쳤네요. 왜 그래요?
마크: 면도하다가 다**친 거예요**.

(2) A: 어, 머리 예쁘다!
B: 지난 달에 한국 갔을 때 파마**한 거야**. — I had a perm when I went to Korea last month.

(3) A: 시험 공부하세요?
B: 아니요. 그냥 책 읽**는 거예요**. — No, I'm just reading a book.

(4) [Seeing someone eating a strange thing]
지금 뭐 먹**는 거예요**? (I recognize you are eating something, but what is it that you are eating?)

Notes

1. ~는/(으)ㄴ 거예요/거야 is used to describe some events or states of affairs in a manner of clarifying or recounting them. It gives an effect of saying 'What it is, is . . .', 'The fact is . . .', or 'What happens is . . .'

2. ~는 and ~(으)ㄴ are the noun-modifying suffixes. 거, contracted from 것, is a noun that means 'a thing, a fact'. It cannot be used by itself, but is always preceded either by a noun-modifying form of a predicate, another noun, or a determiner such as 이, 그, 저, etc.

~는/(으)ㄴ 거예요/거야 is a colloquial form of ~는/(으)ㄴ 것이에요/것이야. ~는/(으)ㄴ 거예요 is in the polite style, and ~는/(으)ㄴ 거야 in the intimate style. The deferential form is ~는/(으)ㄴ 겁니다.

거예요, 거야, and 겁니다 are derived as follows where 이 is the copula 'to be'.

Intimate style:	것 + 이 + 야 > 거야
Polite style:	것 + 이 + 어요 > 거예요
Deferential style:	것 + 이 + ㅂ니다 > 겁니다

Exercises

Using ~는/(으)ㄴ 거예요, clarify the given situations.

(1) A: 머리 너무 예쁘네요.
B: 파마 전문 미용실에서 한 거예요.

(2) A: 와, 예쁘다! 이 옷 어디서 샀어요?
B: ____________________

(3) A: 사람들이 왜 저렇게 모여 있어요?
B: ____________________

(4) 영미: 이 케이크 민지 씨가 가져왔어요?
민지: ____________________

(5) A: 미국에서는 팁을 얼마 줘요?
B: ____________________

G9.4 Causative ~이/~히/~리/~기/~우

Examples

(1) 마크: 요리 잘해요?
동수: 당연히 못 하지요. 어제도 생선을 **태워**서 냄새 때문에 혼났어요. — Of course not. Even yesterday I burned the fish and had an awful time because of the smell.

(2) 민지: 성희야, 요즘 어떻게 지내니?
성희: 아휴, 아기 때문에 너무 바빠.
우유 **먹이**고, 밤에는 자기 전에 옷 **벗기**고 **재우**고 나면 12시야.
또 어디 나가려면 옷 **입히**고 신발 **신기**는 것도 너무 힘들어.

(3) 성희: 민지야, 텔레비전에서 요새 새로 나온 드라마 보니?
민지: 아니. 재미있어?
성희: 응, 사람을 **웃기**기도 하고 **울리**기도 해.

Notes

1. Some verbs express actions that cause someone to do something, or make someone or something go through a change of state. These verbs are called 'causative' verbs, as seen in the above examples.

2. In Korean, these causative verbs are derived from the corresponding non-causative (plain) verbs by adding one of these seven suffixes, ~이, ~히, ~리, ~기, ~우, ~구, and ~추. Note that these suffixes are similar in form to passive suffixes (G6.3).

As in the case of passive verbs, which verb takes which causative suffix has to be learned case by case. In this lesson, we will learn only those verbs that are formed with ~이, ~히, ~리, ~기, and ~우, which are the most common.

Plain	Causative	Example
(i) ~이 types		
먹다 (아이가 우유를 먹어요.)	먹이다 feed someone	아이한테 우유를 먹여요. I feed milk to the baby.
죽다 (벌레가 죽어요.)	죽이다 kill someone/something	벌레를 죽여요. I kill an insect.
끓다 (물이 끓어요.)	끓이다 boil something	물을 끓여요. I boil water.
(ii) ~히 types		
입다 (아이가 옷을 입어요.)	입히다 dress someone	아이에게 옷을 입혀요. I dress the child.
눕다 (아이가 침대에 누워요.)	눕히다 lay someone or something down	아이를 침대에 눕혀요. I lay the baby on the bed.
앉다 (아이가 의자에 앉아요.)	앉히다 seat someone	아이를 의자에 앉혀요. I seat the child on a chair.
(iii) ~리 types		
울다 (아기가 울어요.)	울리다 make someone cry	아기를 울려요. I make the baby cry.
얼다 (물이 얼어요.)	얼리다 freeze something	물을 얼려요. I freeze water.
(iv) ~기 types		
벗다 (아이가 옷을 벗어요.)	벗기다 undress someone	아이의 옷을 벗겨요. I undress the child.
웃다 (아이가 웃어요.)	웃기다 make someone laugh	아이를 웃겨요. I make the child laugh.
신다 (아이가 신을 신어요.)	신기다 put shoes on someone	아이에게 신을 신겨요. I put shoes on the child.
(v) ~우 types		
자다 (아이가 자요.)	재우다 put someone to sleep	아이를 재워요. I put the baby to sleep.
타다 (생선이 타요.)	태우다 burn something	생선을 태워요. I burn the fish.
깨다 (오늘 일찍 깼어요.)	깨우다 wake someone up	엄마가 아이를 깨웠어요. The mom woke the baby up.

Exercises

Fill in the blank with the proper form of a causative verb. Choose from the given list an appropriate verb for the given context.

깨다 타다 울다 먹다 자다 입다 신다 벗다

(1) 마크: 요리 솜씨가 많이 늘었어요?
동수: 아니요, 어제는 갈비를 태웠어요.

(2) A: 아기가 울어요.
B: 배고파서 그래요.
우유를 4시에 ________고 안 ________거든요.
A: 아기 ________지 말고 빨리 우유를 주세요.
아기 오래 울면 안 좋아요.

(3) A: 아기가 자요?
B: 네, 겨우 잠들었어요.
너무 안 자서 ________느라고 힘들었어요.

(4) A: 아기 옷 다 ________________?
B: 아니요, 아직요. 아기가 울어서요.

(5) A: 아기가 왜 안 웃어요?
B: 글쎄요. 졸린가 봐요. 한번 ________ 보세요.

(6) 엄마: 형 일어났니?
폴: 아니요, 아직 자고 있는데요.
엄마: 빨리 가서 ________. 학교 늦었어.

Narration 스티브의 일기 3

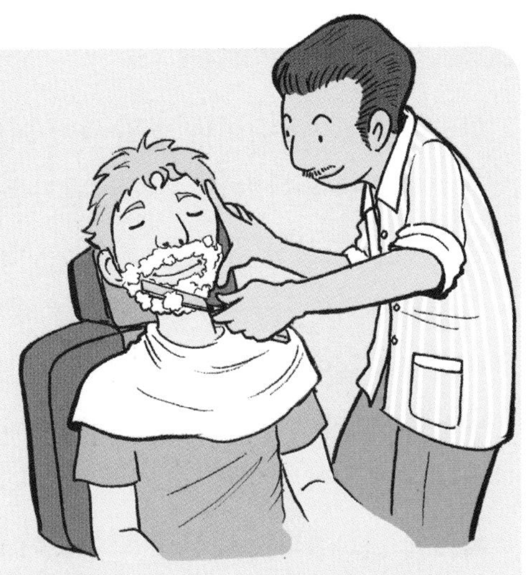

한국에 와서 처음 머리를 깎으러 이발소에 갔다. 한국에서는 요즘 남자들도 미용실에서 머리를 깎는다고 한다. 그런데 나는 이발소에 한번 가 보고 싶어서 동네 이발소에 갔다. 이발사 아저씨는 이 동네에서 30년 동안이나 이발소를 하셨다고 한다. 나는 옆머리와 뒷머리는 짧게 깎고 앞머리도 조금 더 다듬어 달라고 했다. 머리를 다 깎고 나서 보니까 아주 시원해 보여서 좋았다. 머리를 깎고 나서 아저씨가 머리도 감겨 주고 면도까지 해 주셨다. 돈을 내면서 팁을 주려고 했는데 아저씨가 한국에서는 팁을 안 받는다고 하셨다. 아저씨가 아주 친절하게 해 주셔서 또 와야겠다고 생각했다.

COMPREHENSION QUESTIONS

1. 요즘 한국에서는 남자들이 어디서 머리를 깎습니까?
2. 스티브는 어디서 머리를 깎았습니까?
3. 이발사 아저씨는 어떤 사람입니까?
4. 머리를 깎고 나서 무엇을 했습니까?
5. 스티브는 왜 아저씨에게 팁을 안 주었습니까?

CULTURE

이발소와 미용실 Barbershops and Beauty Salons

한국에서는 미용실이나 병원 등에 미리[1] 예약을 하지 않고 그냥 가서 순서[2]를 기다리면 된다. 이발소에는 남자들만 가는데, 그곳에서는 이발과 면도[3]뿐 아니라 마사지[4]와 손톱 손질[5]을 해 주기도 한다. 미용실은 전통적으로 여자들이 가는 곳이었지만 요즘은 젊은 남자들도 커트와 파마 또는 염색을 하러 미용실에 간다. 파마와 염색[6]은 모든 연령대[7]의 여성들뿐 아니라 젊은 남성들에게도 인기[8]가 있다. 이발소나 미용실, 또는 식당에서 팁[9]을 주는 것에는 특별한[10] 규칙[11]이 없다. 한국에서는 헤어스타일의 유행이 굉장히 빠르게 변화한다[12]. 많은 한국인들이 패션에 큰 관심[13]을 갖고 있기 때문에 헤어스타일의 유행에도 민감[14]한 편이다.

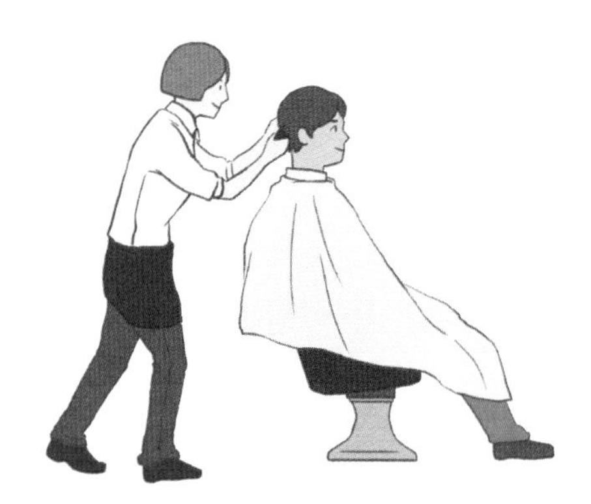

1. 미리: in advance
2. 순서: order, turn
3. 면도: shaving
4. 마사지: massage
5. 손톱 손질: manicure
6. 염색하다: to dye
7. 연령대: age group
8. 인기: popularity
9. 팁: tip
10. 특별하다: be special
11. 규칙: regulations
12. 변화하다: to change
13. 관심: interest, concern
14. 민감하다: be sensitive

USAGE

1 *Describing hairstyles and hair fashions*

Take the roles of a customer and a hairdresser, and practice with your classmate.

(1) 이발사: 손님, 이리로 앉으세요.
머리 어떻게 깎아 드릴까요?
손님: 조금 다듬어 주세요.
뒷머리는 짧게 깎고
앞머리는 조금만 깎아 주세요.
이발사: 옆머리는 어떻게 해 드릴까요?
손님: 조금만 잘라 주세요.
이발사: 네, 알겠습니다.

(2) 미용사: 머리 어떻게 해 드릴까요?
손님: 좀 다듬고 파마하려고 해요.
미용사: 어떤 스타일을 원하세요?
손님: 좀 굵게, 자연스럽게 해 주세요.

Exercise 1

Practice the conversation above again with each of the following changes.

(1) A customer wants to have a simple trim.
(2) A customer wants to have a new hairstyle.
(3) A customer wants to have a short hair perm.
(4) A customer wants to have a natural-looking perm.

(Variation: After having a haircut or a perm, each customer above is asking the question "이 머리 어떻게 손질해야 되나요?" to the hairdresser. Take the role of the hairdresser and make some suggestions to the customer. Some possible answers are as follows.)

머리 감고 나서 무스를 살짝 발라 주세요.
그냥 빗으로 빗으면 돼요.
드라이로 말리면서 빗으로 빗으면 돼요.
앞머리에 젤(gel)을 조금 발라 주시면 돼요.

Useful expressions

(머리) 다듬다	'to trim'
(머리) 빗	'a comb'
머리를 깎다/자르다	'to have a haircut'
머리를 빗다	'to comb'
이발하다	(men only) 'to have a haircut'
머리를 감다	'to wash hair'
샴푸하다	'to shampoo'
머리를 말리다	'to dry hair'
드라이하다	'to dry hair with a hair dryer'
파마하다	'to get a perm'
굵은 파마	'a perm with large rollers'
유행하는 파마	'a trendy perm'
젤을 바르다	'to apply gel'

Exercise 2

Converse with your partner using the following questions.

(1) 머리 얼마나 자주 깎으세요/자르세요?
(2) 머리 깎으러/깎으러 보통 어디 가세요?
(3) 왜 거기 가세요?
(4) 머리 깎은/자른 지 얼마나 됐어요?
(5) 머리 말릴 때 드라이로 말리세요?
(6) 머리 감고 나서 무스를 바르세요?
(7) 어떤 헤어 스타일을 좋아하세요?

(Variation: Write the answers and report them to your class.)

2 *Commenting on someone's appearance*

Upon greeting each other, Koreans often comment on the other person's physical appearance (particularly among friends). In the following dialogue, Minji and Steve meet after a long time and talk about each other's appearance.

민지:	스티브 씨, 오래간만이에요. 그동안 잘 지내셨어요? 얼굴이 좋아 보이시네요.
스티브:	민지 씨도 헤어스타일이 바뀐 것 같은데요?
민지:	네, 조금 바꿔 봤어요.
스티브:	보기 좋은데요. 민지 씨 얼굴하고 잘 어울리는 것 같아요.
민지:	아, 그래요? 스티브 씨도 더 젊어지셨어요.

Exercise 1

It is the first day of Korean class following a winter break. There are changes in physical appearance among the students. Pair up, with one person taking the role of each student below, and the other person commenting on the change.

Students	Changes
민지	Her new outfit looks great.
유진	He dyed his hair.
샌디	She has lost weight.
마크	His hairstyle has changed.

Useful expressions

좋아 보이시네요.
더 어려 보이는데요.
살이 빠진 것 같은데요.
예뻐지셨어요.
헤어스타일이 바뀌셨네요.
옷이 참 잘 어울리네요.
넥타이 참 멋있네요.
머리 염색하셨네요. (염색하다 to dye)

Exercise 2

Koreans tend to politely deflect compliments they receive from others (except between intimate friends). Make a dialogue between two acquaintances with one person giving the following compliments to the other.

(1) "Your new hairstyle looks great on you."
(2) "You got younger and prettier."
(3) "You look slimmer."

3 *Reading and making ads*

Read the following ad and answer the questions.

미나 미용실

남녀 헤어컷
스페셜 파마 전문
상한 머리를 부드럽고 윤기 있는
머리로 만들어 드립니다.
스킨 케어

헤어컷:	삼만 원
파마:	칠만 원 (짧은 머리),
	십만 (긴 머리)
전화 예약:	654-1280
	월요일-금요일 10-7pm
	토요일-일요일 10-9pm
주소:	지하철 이대역 출구 옆

매달 셋째 월요일은 쉽니다.

Exercise 1

Exchange the following information with your partner in Korean.

(1) How much is a perm for short hair?
(2) How much is a haircut?
(3) When does the beauty salon close?
(4) Where is the shop located?

Exercise 2

Make an advertisement for your favorite beauty shop or barbershop.

Notes

Lesson 9. Beauty Salons and Barbershops

CONVERSATION 1 *Please Make It Natural*

Minji went to a hair salon to get her hair permed.

Clerk:	Hi, welcome. Did you make an appointment?
Minji:	Yes, I had one at three.
Clerk:	Oh, Miss Minji Kim, I see your appointment at three here. Please sit down here.
	(A little later)
Hairdresser:	How would you like your hair done?
Minji:	I want to get my hair permed.
Hairdresser:	What kind of style do you want?
Minji:	Please make it look natural with waves and big curls.
Hairdresser:	How much should I cut?
Minji:	Just cut my bangs a little bit shorter.
Hairdresser:	Do you want me to trim your hair in the back as well?
Minji:	Yes, please.
	(Two hours later, her hair is finished.)
Hairdresser:	How is it? Do you like it?
Minji:	Yes, it's very pretty. But how do I do this hairstyle?
Hairdresser:	You should just need to blow-dry it a little after shampooing.
Minji:	Okay, I see. Thank you.

CONVERSATION 2 *How Would You Like Your Hair Cut?*

Steve went to a barbershop to get his hair cut.

Barber:	How would you like your hair cut?
Steve:	Just tidy it up a bit, please.
Barber:	Your hair is pretty long. How long has it been since you last got your hair cut?
Steve:	I think it's been about three months.
Barber:	You haven't cut your hair for three whole months?
Steve:	It's just such a pain in the neck to get a haircut. This is the first time I'm getting it cut since I came to Korea.
Barber:	Oh, really?

	(A little later)
Barber:	How are the sides? Do you want them a bit shorter?
Steve:	Yes, and please cut a little more off my bangs too. They look a little long.
Barber:	Okay, will do.
	(A little later)
Barber:	I will wash your hair over there.
	(After his hair is washed.)
Barber:	Do you like it?
Steve:	Yes, it looks nice. Thank you.

NARRATION *Steve's Diary 3*

I went to a barbershop to get a haircut for the first time since I came to Korea. I heard that lately, men in Korea also go to get their hair cut in hair salons. But I wanted to try a barbershop, so I went to one in my neighborhood. The barber told me he has been running the barbershop for thirty years in this neighborhood. I asked him to cut the sides and back short and just trim the front. After the haircut, I liked it since my hair looked neat and felt light. He also washed my hair and shaved my beard after the haircut. I wanted to leave a tip when paying, but he said they don't receive tips in Korea. I thought to myself that I should return because the barber was so kind.

CULTURE *Barbershops and Beauty Parlors*

In Korea, people aren't required to make appointments in advance at places like beauty parlors or hospitals, they can simply enter and wait in line to be helped. Barbershops are places where only men go; they don't only give haircuts and shaves, but also provide manicures and massages. Beauty parlors are traditionally places where only women patronize; however lately young men also go to beauty parlors for haircuts, perms, and even hair coloring. Perms and hair dyes are popular not only for women of all ages, but also for young men as well. There are no special rules for giving tips at barbershops, beauty parlors, or even at restaurants. In Korea, hairstyle trends change very rapidly. Many Koreans tend to be sensitive to these hairstyle trends because so many of them have a deep interest in fashion.

esc
Q W E R T Y U
A S D F G H J
Z X C V B N
fn ctrl alt cmd

10과 취미 생활

Lesson 10 Hobbies

Conversation 1 시간 있을 때 주로 뭐 하세요?

Conversation 1

소연: 유진 씨는 시간 있을 때 주로 뭐 하세요?
유진: 운동도 하고 영화도 보고 그래요. 소연 씨는요?
소연: 저는 콘서트에 자주 가요. 콘서트에 가면 스트레스가 다 풀리거든요.
유진: 아, 그래요? 저는 운동을 해서 스트레스를 푸는 편이에요.
소연: 운동 경기 보는 것도 좋아하세요?
유진: 네, 가끔 경기장에도 가요.
소연: 경기장에 가면 더 재미있어요?
유진: 그럼요, 지난주에는 친구들하고 야구장에 갔다가[G10.1] 제가 홈런볼을 잡았어요.
소연: 정말이요?
유진: 네, 경기 끝나고 나서 홈런 친 선수가 야구공에 직접 사인도 해 주고 사진도 같이 찍어 주더라고요.[G10.2]
소연: 와! 정말 좋았겠네요.
유진: 소연 씨도 다음에 같이 한번 가요.

COMPREHENSION QUESTIONS

1. 유진이는 시간이 있을 때 주로 무엇을 합니까?
2. 소연이는 시간이 있을 때 주로 무엇을 합니까?
3. 유진이는 지난주에 무엇을 했습니까?
4. 어떤 재미있는 일이 있었습니까?

NEW WORDS

NOUN

경기장	sports stadium
경험(하다)	experience
공짜	free
마지막	last
매달	every month
배우	actor
사인	signature
상품	prize; merchandise
선수	athlete
씨름	Korean wrestling
여가	free time
야구공	baseball
직장	workplace
할인	discount
홈런볼	home run ball

NOUN SUFFIX

씩	each, apiece

VERB

(시간을) 내다	to make time
부르다	to call out
(스트레스) 쌓이다	be piled up
잡다	to catch
타다	to win (a prize)
풀리다	to be relieved

CONJUNCTIVE

그러니까	so

ADJECTIVE

날씬하다	be slim
상쾌하다	be refreshing
이르다	be early

SUFFIX

~더라고요	speaker's past experience
~었/았다가	change in momentum

NEW EXPRESSIONS

Both 콘서트 and 음악회 mean 'concert'. However, in general, 콘서트 is used for pop music whereas 음악회 is used for classical music.

Grammar

G10.1 Expressing change in momentum: ~었/았다(가)

Examples

(1) 소연: 성희가 어제 씨름 구경 **갔다(가)** 공짜로 텔레비전을 탔대요.
유진: 정말이에요? 좋아하는 씨름도 보고 상품도 타고,
성희 씨 좋은 경험했네요.

(2) 성희: 유진아, 요새 테니스 안 쳐?
유진: 응. 지난번에 오랜만에 테니스 **쳤다(가)** 다리가 아파서
혼났어.
성희: 그러니까 자주 쳐야지.

(3) 동수: 마크 씨는 학교에 뭐 타고 와요?
마크: 버스 타고 와요.
동수: 지하철 안 타요?
마크: 지난번에 지하철 **탔다(가)** 사람 많아서 혼났어요.

(4) A: 나 잠깐 **나갔다(가)** 올게. — I'm going out and will be back in a little while.
B: 그럼, 집에 오는 길에 슈퍼에 좀 들**렀다(가)** 올래? — Then, on your way home, (can you) stop at the supermarket?

Notes

1. Recall that ~다(가) indicates that momentum is transferred or shifted from one action or state to another. It was noted that the new action or state occurs in the middle of the earlier action or state.

2. ~었/았다(가) expresses that momentum is shifted only after the earlier action has been completed rather than in the middle of it. Compare:

(i) 학교에 가다가 샌디를 만났다.
(ii) 학교에 갔다가 샌디를 만났다.

In (i), the speaker met 샌디 on his/her way to school. In (ii), on the other hand, the speaker met 샌디 after arriving at school.

3. Often ~(었/았)다가 is used without 가.

4. Some commonly used expressions with ~었다(가):

> 이번 주에는 여행갔다(가) 오느라고 수영을 한 번도 못 갔어요.
> [갔다(가) 오다 (*lit*. to come back after having gone)]
>
> 요즘 날씨가 추웠다(가) 더웠다(가) 해서 감기 들기 쉬워요.
> [추웠다(가) 더웠다(가): description of fickle weather]
>
> 요새 눈이 너무 많이 와서 왔다갔다 하기가 불편해요
> [왔다갔다 하다 to come and go, back and forth, move around]

For these expressions, ~었다 without 가 is more commonly used, and in fact, those fixed expressions such as 이랬다 저랬다 and 왔다갔다, 가 are obligatorily omitted.

Exercises

Using ~었/았다가, fill in the blanks.

(1) 성희: 유진아, 요새 테니스 안 쳐?
유진: 응. <u>지난번에 오랜만에 테니스 쳤다가</u> 다리가 아파서 혼났어. 그래서 요즘 조금 쉬고 있는 중이야.

(2) A: 샌디 봤어요?
B: 네, 아까 ________________ 도서관 앞에서 만났어요.

(3) A: 늦었는데 우리 택시 타고 갈까요?
B: 지금 시간에는 지하철이 빨라요.
지난번에 ____________________길이 막혀서
1시간이나 늦었어요.

(4) A: 우리 영화 보러 안 갈래요?
B: 안 돼요. 지난번에 ____________________
아버지한테 혼났어요.
(한테 혼나다 to be scolded by . . .)

(5) A: 식당에 예약 안 해도 되지요?
B: 아니요, 예약해야 돼요. 지난번에
________________________ 자리가 없어서 저녁을 못 먹었어요.

G10.2 Expressing the speaker's past experience: ~더라고(요)

Examples

(1) 소연: 어제 씨름 구경 갔다가 공짜로 핸드폰을 탔어요.
유진: 정말이요?
소연: 네. 경기 끝나고 나오는데 제 티켓 번호를 부르**더라고요**.
그래서 가니까 핸드폰을 공짜로 주던데요.

(2) 성희: 소연아, 너 요새 날씬해졌다.
소연: 응, 요새 매일 수영하거든.
수영하니까 운동도 되고 취미생활도 되고,
스트레스 쌓일 때도 좋**더라고**.

(3) 유진: 아직은 좀 이른데 점심 먹으러 갈까요?
성희: 학교 앞에 한식집으로 가요. 지난번에 11시쯤 갔었는데
사람들이 많이 와 있**더라고요**.

Notes

1. Recall that ~더 is used to describe a situation in the past when the speaker experienced that situation. Combined together, ~더라고(요) is used to report, in the self-quotation form, the speaker's own past experience about a situation he/she happened to witness or experience in a moment in the past.

2. The self-quotation form ~라고(요) is used to emphasize the validity of the report; the speaker has the authority because it is his/her experience. It gives an effect of saying 'I am telling you' or 'Let me tell you'.

Exercises

Using ~더라고(요), complete the dialogue in which the speaker reports his/her past experience and emphasizes its validity in the sense of 'I am telling you' or 'Let me tell you'.

(1) A: 이번 토요일에 박물관에 같이 갈래요?
B: 일요일은 어때요?
A: 매달 마지막 토요일에 할인을 해 주더라고요.

(2) A: 어제 농구 경기 보셨어요?
B: 네, 봤어요. LA 레이커스가 정말 ________________.

(3) A: 여가를 어떻게 보내세요?
B: 지난 달부터 골프를 치는데 ________________.
그래서 요즘 거의 매일 쳐요.

(4) A: 요즘도 야구 보러 다니세요?
B: 아니요. 직장 생활을 하니까 시간 내기가
________________.

(5) A: 수영하러 자주 가?
B: 응, 일주일에 두 번씩 하는데 기분도 상쾌하고
________________.

(6) A: 한국 영화 배우 직접 본 적 있어요?
B: 네. 작년에 한국 갔을 때 이병헌을 본 적이 있는데
________________.

Conversation 2 어떤 프로그램을 자주 보니?

영진이 운전하는 차 안에서

Conversation 2

영진: 아, 졸려 죽겠다.[G10.3] 소연아, 라디오 좀 틀어 줄래?

소연: 응, 그래. 마침 내가 좋아하는 노래가 나오네.

영진: 이제 잠이 좀 깨는 것 같다.

소연: 이게 요즘 가장 인기 있는 노래야.

영진: 근데 나는 요새 새로 나오는 노래는 하나도 모르겠던데. 너는 음악 프로 자주 보니?

소연: 가끔 보기도 하는데[G10.4] 주로 인터넷으로 찾아 보는 편이야.

영진: 나는 예능 프로를 자주 봐. 근데 지난 일요일에는 예능 프로 때문에 동생하고 싸웠어.

소연: 왜?

영진: 걔는 스포츠를 좋아하는데 축구 경기 시간이랑 겹쳤거든. 그래서 걔가 경기 보는 중간에 내가 채널을 돌려 버렸어.[G10.5]

소연: 뭐 그런 걸로 싸우니.

COMPREHENSION QUESTIONS

1. 소연이는 주로 어떤 티비 프로를 보는 편입니까?
2. 영진이는 어떤 티비 프로를 자주 봅니까?
3. 영진이는 왜 동생하고 자주 싸우게 됩니까?

NEW WORDS

NOUN

감상(하다)	appreciation
걔	that kid
계절 학기	summer/winter term
동호회	(amateur) club
모기	mosquito
예능	entertainment
월급	salary
정보	information
채널	channel
출근(하다)	going to work
퇴근(하다)	leaving work
티비	TV
프로(그램)	program
학점	(school) credit

ADJECTIVE

다양하다	be diverse
새롭다	be new, original
커다랗다	be large, huge

VERB

겹치다	to overlap
돌리다	to change (the channel)
틀다	to turn on (electronics)
새우다 (밤을)	to stay up all night
쓰러지다	to collapse
얻다	to gain

ADVERB

아무리	no matter how
언제나	all the time
점점	gradually
하나도	not even one

PARTICLE

(이)랑	and, with (for people)

SUFFIX

~기도 하다	sometimes . . . too
~어/아 버리다	do completely
~어/아 죽겠다	. . . to death

NEW EXPRESSIONS

1. 걔 is a contracted form of 그 아이 'that kid', which is very casual form used with a child or close childhood friend.

얘 (이 아이)	걔 (그 아이)	쟤 (저 아이)

2. 채널을 돌리다 'to change the TV channel'
   라디오를 틀다 'to turn on the radio'

Grammar

G10.3 ~어/아(서) 죽겠다 '. . . to death'

Examples

(1) 영진: 소연아, 졸**려 죽겠는데** 라디오 좀 틀어 줄래?
소연: 그래. 마침 신나는 노래가 나오네.

(2) 유진: 소연 씨, 점심 먹으러 안 갈래요? 배고**파 죽겠어요**. — Soyeon, don't you want to go eat lunch? I'm starving to death.
소연: 지금 12시밖에 안 됐는데, 오늘 아침 안 먹었어요?

(3) A: 날씨가 너무 더워서 목말**라 죽겠다**.
B: 많이 덥지? 이 물 마셔.

(4) A: 새로 이사 간 집 어때요?
B: 옆집 아이가 너무 울어서 시끄러**워 죽겠어요**.

Notes

1. ~어/아(서) 죽겠다, literally meaning 'so . . . that I would die', indicates that the state of affairs described is unbearable; best translated as '. . . to death'.

2. The expression may be preceded by a statement of why such an unbearable state has been reached, as in (3) and (4). The preceding statement often contains the expression 하도 ~어서, which means that the degree of the situation has reached its maximum.

Exercises

Complete the given utterance with an expression that indicates that the state of affairs described is unbearable.

(1) A: (Seeing B scratching his arm) 왜 그래요?
B: 모기가 물었나 봐요. 가려워('itchy') 죽겠어요.

(2) A: 어디 아파요?
B: 배가 ____________________. 어제 첫 월급 받아서 친구들이랑 저녁을 두 번이나 먹었거든요.

(3) A: 어제 잠 못 잤어요?
B: 네, ____________________. 오늘 시험이 있어서 밤을 새웠거든요.

(4) A: 한국어 공부하기 어때요?
B: 아무리 공부해도 점점 더 어려워져요. ____________________.

(5) A: 한 시간이나 걸었는데 괜찮아? 난 피곤해서 쓰러지겠어.
B: 나도 ____________________.

Notes

G10.4 ~기도 하다 'sometimes . . . too'

Examples

(1) 민지: 민지랑 동수가 잘 어울리죠?
마크: 네. 근데, 두 사람 성격이 너무 달라서 데이트할 때 가끔 싸우**기도 한**대요. — Yes, but when they were dating, they said they also occasionally fought.

(2) 마크: 특별한 취미가 있으세요?
민지: 영화 감상을 좋아해요. 요즘은 동호회에서 새롭고 다양한 정보를 얻**기도 해요**. — I like watching movies. These days, I also gain various new information from the movie clubs.

(3) 마크: 한국에서는 대학생들이 여름 방학 때 보통 뭐 해요?
민지: 보통은 여행을 많이 하는데 취미 생활이나 아르바이트를 하**기도 해요**. 학점이 필요한 학생들은 계절 학기 수업을 듣**기도 하고요**.

(4) 수연: 퇴근하면 보통 뭐 하세요?
동수 : 소설을 읽**기도 하고**, 볼링을 치**기도 하고**, 친구도 만나고 그래요.

Notes

~기도 하다, where ~기 changes a predicate into a noun and 도 means 'also', indicates that the given action or practice is also a possibility in addition to what is mentioned or suggested in the preceding context. It is typically used when the speaker adds a less common practice to a more popular one.

Exercises

Using ~기도 하다, complete the dialogues with an expression with which the speaker adds another possibility to a more common practice.

(1) 영진: 요즘은 어떤 동호회에 나가세요?
소연: 사진 동호회에 나가는데 가끔 만나서
식사를 하기도 해요.

(2) 마크: 보통 점심 때 뭐 먹어요?
민지: 보통 샌드위치나 피자를 먹어요.
그런데 친구를 만날 때는
______________________.

(3) 성희: 스티브 씨는 주말에 보통 뭐 해요?
스티브: 보통은 집에서 책을 보거나 자요.
가끔 심심하면 ______________________________.

(4) 민지: 마크 씨, 호주에서는 학교에 어떻게 다녀요?
마크: 보통 학교 근처에서 살기 때문에, 언제나 자전거를
타고 다녀요. 가끔 비가 오거나 날씨가 추우면
________________________.

(5) 성희: 여름 방학 때 주로 뭐 하세요?
스티브: 여행을 가기도 하고 ___________________________.

Notes

G10.5 ~어/아 버리다 'do completely'

Examples

(1) 오늘 먹으려고 했던 케이크를 남동생이 다 먹**어 버렸다**. — My younger brother ate up all the cake that I had purposely left to eat today.

(2) 마크: 소연 씨, 백화점에서 세일하는데 같이 쇼핑하러 갈래요?
소연: 아, 저는 컴퓨터 사느라고 돈을 다 **써 버려서** 쇼핑은 못 해요.

(3) 민지: 동수한테 전화해 줬어?
성희: 아니, 오늘 너무 바빠서 잊**어버렸어**.

(4) 소연: 유진 씨, 한국어 숙제 같이 할래요?
유진: 저는 벌써 다 끝**내 버렸어요**.

Notes

1. 버리다 means 'throw away (an object)'. For example,

민호는 휴지를 휴지통에 버렸다. — Minho threw the trash into the trash can.

When you throw something away, the physical effect is that the entity disappears and nothing is left. The emotional effect of this is twofold, depending on your expectation or desire about the entity. If the entity that has been thrown away is something that you wanted to keep, the effect of its being thrown away or disappearing is regret. However, if it is something you wanted to get rid of, then the effect of its being thrown away is relief.

~어/아 버리다, literally meaning 'throw away an action of ~', is used to refer to the emotional effect of swiftly finishing or cleaning up something. Thus, it has the meaning of 'to do completely', 'to get it done', or 'to do it all (away, up, etc.)'. In (1) through (3), the emotional effect of the action is regret, disappointment, or feeling of emptiness. In (4), the emotional effect is relief.

2. There are formulaic expressions which the meaning of regret is built into.

잊어버리다: 오늘 시험 있는 걸 잊어버렸어요.
잃어버리다: 오늘 길에서 지갑을 잃어버렸어요.

Exercises

Using ~어/아 버리다, complete the given utterance or sentence with an expression that would connote regret or disappointment.

(1) 제니: 어제 데이트 잘 했어요?
마크: 저녁 먹다가 싸워서 여자 친구가 집에 그냥 가 버렸어요. (go)

(2) A: 어제 드라마 봤어요?
B: 좀 보다가 재미없어서 채널을 ____________________ (switch, change)

(3) A: (냉장고 문을 열어 보고) 어제 산 수박 어디 갔어?
B: 내가 다 ____________________ (eat), 어떡하지?
A: 그 커다란 걸 혼자 다 먹었어?
B: 미안해.
A: 아니, 괜찮아.

(4) 민지: (민지 knows that 수연 had an argument with her husband.) 어제 어떻게 됐어요?
수연: 기분이 나빠서 그냥 ____________________ (sleep). 아침에 일어나니까 벌써 출근하고 없더라고요.

(5) A: 머리 스타일이 달라졌네요.
B: 네, 너무 더워서 ____________________(cut).

Narration 현대인의 취미 생활

현대인들은 다양한 취미 생활을 한다. 어떤 사람들은 독서를 하고 어떤 사람들은 음악 감상이나 영화 감상을 한다. 사진 찍는 것을 좋아하는 사람도 있고 운동을 열심히 하는 사람도 있다. 시간을 내어 여행이나 등산을 하는 사람도 있다. 직장에 다니는 사람들은 퇴근 후에 요리나 외국어 등을 배우기도 한다. 또 인터넷 동호회에서 정보를 얻기도 하고 다양한 사람을 만나기도 한다.

현대 생활은 바쁘지만 시간을 내어 좋아하는 일을 하는 것이 중요하다. 좋아하는 일을 하면서 스트레스를 풀 수도 있고, 새로운 것을 경험할 수도 있기 때문이다.

COMPREHENSION QUESTIONS

1. 현대인들은 어떤 취미를 갖고 있습니까?
2. 취미로 어떤 것을 배우기도 합니까?
3. 인터넷 동호회는 무엇입니까?
4. 취미 생활이 왜 필요합니까?

NEW EXPRESSIONS

1. 현대인: 현대 'modern times', 인 'a person'. 현대 생활 'present-day life', 현대 문학 'modern literature'. Words with 인 include 미국인, 영국인, 한국인, 동양인, and 서양인.

2. 생활 refers to actual living and lifestyle (it is not about the state of being alive), as in 여가생활 'leisure activities', 취미생활 'hobbies', 학교생활 'school life'.

3. 감상 'appreciation, enjoyment' as in 영화감상, 음악감상, 미술감상, etc.

Notes

CULTURE

씨름 Ssireum (Korean Wrestling)

씨름은 천 년도 넘은 한국의 전통 레슬링이다. 음력[1] 5월 5일 단오[2]에는 다른 여러 놀이와 함께 항상 씨름 대회가 열렸다. 씨름 우승자[3]는 '세상에서 가장 강한[4] 인간'이라는 뜻의 '천하장사'라고 불렸고[5] 상[6]으로 황소[7] 한 마리를 받았다. 요즘 씨름은 국가적[8]인 스포츠가 되었고, 텔레비전에도 자주 방송된다[9]. 씨름은 양측[10] 선수가 모래[11]에 앉아서 서로의 샅바를 잡으면서 시작된다. 샅바는 허리[12]와 오른쪽 허벅지[13]를 두르고 있는 긴 천[14]을 가리키는 말이다. 상대편[15] 선수가 발이 아닌 다른 신체부위[16]로 모래 바닥[17]을 건드리게[18] 되면 점수를 얻는다.

1. 음력: lunar calendar
2. 단오: Dano day
3. 우승자: the winner
4. 강하다: be strong
5. 불리다: be called
6. 상: award
7. 황소: bull, ox
8. 국가적: national
9. 방송되다: be aired
10. 양측: both parties
11. 모래: sand
12. 허리: waist
13. 허벅지: thigh
14. 천: textile
15. 상대편: opponent
16. 신체부위: body parts
17. 바닥: floor
18. 건드리다: to touch

USAGE

1 *Talking about stressful events*

Practice the following dialogue.

스티브:	요즘 시험 때문에 스트레스가 많아 죽겠어요. 민지 씨는 스트레스가 쌓일 때 어떻게 풀어요?
민지:	주로 수영해요. 수영을 하고 나면 몸도 마음도 가벼워지거든요. 스티브 씨는 어떻게 스트레스를 푸세요?
스티브:	저는 혼자 여행 가는 걸 좋아해요. 그래서 이번 시험이 다 끝나면 여행이나 갔다 올까 해요.
민지:	그거 좋은 생각이네요. 여행을 갔다 오면 쌓였던 스트레스가 다 풀릴 거예요.
스티브:	민지 씨는 언제 스트레스를 받으세요?
민지:	저는 시간은 없고 할 일은 너무 많을 때 스트레스를 받아요.

Useful expressions

스트레스를 느끼다/받다	to feel stress
스트레스가 많다/없다	to have a lot/no stress
스트레스가 쌓이다	(stress) to be accumulated
스트레스를 풀다	to relieve stress
스트레스가 풀리다	(stress) to be relieved

Exercise 1

Interview your classmates using the following questions and report the results to the class in Korean.

(1) 스트레스가 쌓일 때 어떻게 풀어요?
(2) 보통 언제 스트레스를 받으세요?
(3) 지금까지 살아 오면서 스트레스를 가장 많이 받았던 때가 언제였어요? 어떻게 그 스트레스를 풀었어요?
(4) 최근에 스트레스를 받아 본 적이 있으세요? 어떤 스트레스를 받았어요?
(5) 스트레스를 받지 않으려면 어떻게 하는 게 좋을까요?

Exercise 2

아래 사람들 중에서 누가 제일 스트레스가 많다고 생각하세요? 왜요? (Who do you think below is in the most stressful situation? Can you explain the reason? Please put numbers in order of the most stressful to the least stressful. Discuss the results with your classmates.)

이름	Stressful events
수잔	최근에 어머니가 갑자기 돌아가셨다. 어머니는 보통 때 아주 건강하신 편이었다.
영미	한 달 후에 대학교를 졸업하는데 졸업 후 뭘 할지 아직 못 정했다.
철수	담배를 끊은 지 한 달 사이에 몸무게가 10파운드나 늘었다. (몸무게가 늘다 to gain weight)
민호	제일 친한 친구가 오토바이를 타고 가다가 교통사고로 죽었다.
상철	대학 졸업 후 법대에 가고 싶은데 정치학 과목에서 F를 받았다. (법대 law school)
소연	4년 동안 사귀던 남자 친구가 갑자기 헤어지자고 말했다.
영미	라스베가스에 놀러 가서 돈을 1,000불을 잃었는데, 집으로 돌아오는 길에 다른 차를 심하게 박았다. 차 보험이 없다. (박다 to crash, 보험 insurance)

Exercise 3

Give advice or encouragement to each of the above characters.

Exercise 4

Role-play for the following situations:

(1) You are talking with a Korean friend who studies in the United States. Your friend feels very lonely and stressed in having to study abroad all alone. Encourage the friend and give some advice.

(2) Your friend tends to drink alcohol whenever he/she is under stress. Discourage him/her from this habit by saying that alcohol does not help, but it actually causes more stress to your body. Suggest some physical exercise instead.

Exercise 5

How would you deal with the following stressful situations? Pair up with another student and play one of the roles described below. Describe your situation and let the other student play the role of the advisor.

(1) You have to give an oral presentation. You feel you are not prepared at all.

(2) You have a blind date with someone.

(3) You have just failed your first driving test.

(4) You have surgery.

2 *Talking about hobbies and pastimes*

Practice the following conversation. (Use your real names when you practice with a partner.)

동수: 시간 있을 때 주로 뭐 하세요?
소연: 그냥 텔레비전 보면서 쉬는 걸 좋아해요. 동수 씨는요?
동수: 전 볼링 치는 걸 좋아해요.
소연: 볼링 잘 치세요?
동수: 아니요, 뭐 별로 . . . 그저 그래요.
소연: 주말엔 보통 뭐 하세요?
동수: 영화 보러 가기도 하고 친구도 만나요.
소연: 영화 보러 자주 가세요?
동수: 네, 자주 보는 편이에요.

여가 활동 (Spare time activities)

비디오 보다 to watch a video, 오페라를 보다 to see an opera, 소설을 읽다 to read a novel, 그림을 그리다 to draw a picture, 음악 감상 to listen to music, 독서하다 to read

운동 (Sports)

농구 basketball, 배구 volleyball, 축구 soccer, 야구 baseball, 탁구 Ping-Pong, 볼링 치다 bowling, 골프 치다 golf, 씨름 traditional Korean wrestling, 레슬링 wrestling, 낚시 fishing, 등산하다 hiking

More vocabulary for skills and hobbies

잘해요/잘하는 편이에요.	to be good at, skillful at
잘 못해요.	not to be very good at
조금/약간 해요.	can do just a little bit
그저 그래요.	just so-so
잘하지는 못하지만 좋아하는 편이에요.	cannot do very well, but be fond of . . .

Exercise 1

Interview three people for the following questions and report the answers to the class.

(1) 시간 있을 때 보통 뭐 하는 걸 좋아하세요?
(Use the form ~도 하고 ~도 하다 in the answer.)
(2) 주말엔 보통 뭐 하세요?
(3) 앞으로 시간과 돈이 더 있다면 어떤 취미생활을 하고 싶으세요?
(4) 제일 좋아하는 운동이 뭐예요?
어느 팀 (team)과 선수 (player)를 좋아하세요?

Useful expressions

(1) 그림 그리다	(2) 피아노 치다	(3) 골프 치다	(4) 낚시하다
(5) 농구하다	(6) 수영하다	(7) 태권도 하다	(8) 축구하다

Exercise 2

Role play

(1) You are taking five courses this quarter and also work fifteen hours a week at a school library. Your friend graduated from school last year and works full-time at a company. His boss is very demanding and unpredictable. Talk about each other's stress and pastimes.

(2) You would like to go hiking with a friend this Saturday. Call and make the necessary arrangements with the friend.

(3) You would like to go out with a woman who lives in the same apartment building as you. Find out her interests or hobbies, and ask her for a date.

Exercise 3

Write about your favorite hobby and report it to the class.

3 *Reporting one's past experiences*

In pairs, practice the following conversation.

(1) 소연: 그저께 씨름 구경 갔다가 공짜로 텔레비전을 탔어요.
유진: 정말이요?
소연: 네, 경기 끝나고 나오는데, 마이크에서 제 입장권 번호를 부르더라고요. 그래서 가니까 텔레비전을 공짜로 주던데요.
유진: 좋아하는 씨름도 보고 상품도 타고, 신났겠네요.

(2) Steve is talking with Youngmee about his experiences in Korea.

영미: 마크 씨, 정말 오래간만이에요. 지난주에 돌아왔다면서요? 한국 생활은 어땠어요?
마크: 재미있었어요. 처음엔 힘들었는데 나중엔 거기서 사귄 친구들하고 아주 친하게 지냈어요. 여행도 같이 많이 다녔어요.
영미: 불편한 점은 없었어요?
스티브: 신발을 벗고 방안에 들어가는 게 좀 불편했었는데 곧 익숙해지더라구요.

Exercise 1

Practice the conversation (1) again by changing 씨름 to the following.

(1) 태권도 (2) 레슬링 (3) 야구 (4) 농구

Exercise 2

Converse with your friend on the following past experiences and report the results to the class.

(1) the most memorable trip
(2) prom in high school
(3) experiences in Korean culture
(4) an unusual part-time job
(5) the most memorable holiday
(6) the most stressful event

Exercise 3

Role play

(1) You run into an old friend from elementary school at a supermarket. Talk to him/her about the past years and things you have done during that period.

(2) You run into a classmate from Korean class ten years from now on a subway in New York. Exchange information about what you have been doing during the past ten years.

(3) You just returned to the United States after studying in Seoul for one year as an exchange student. Your classmate is considering going to Korea next summer to teach English and wants to know more about Korea. Describe your past experiences in Seoul.

Lesson 10 Hobbies

CONVERSATION 1 *What Do You Normally Do When You Have Time?*

Soyeon: Yujin, what do you usually do when you have free time?
Yujin: I normally work out or watch movies. What about you, Soyeon?
Soyeon: I usually go to concerts, because going to concerts relieves all my stress.
Yujin: Oh really? I work out, and that tends to relieve my stress.
Soyeon: Do you like watching sports too?
Yujin: Yeah, I even go to the stadium sometimes.
Soyeon: Is it more fun when you actually go to the stadium?
Yujin: Of course. Last week I went to a baseball game with some friends and I caught a home run ball.
Soyeon: Really?
Yujin: Yes, and once the game ended, the player who hit the home run personally autographed the ball and took a picture with me.
Soyeon: Wow, that must have been really nice.
Yujin: Let's go together next time, Soyeon.

CONVERSATION 2 *What TV Programs Do You Watch?*

In the car while Youngjin is driving

Youngjin: Ugh, I'm so tired I could die. Soyeon, can you turn the radio on?
Soyeon: Sure. Hey, they're even playing a song I like.
Youngjin: I feel like I'm waking up a bit now.
Soyeon: This is the most popular song nowadays.
Youngjin: Huh, I don't know any new songs that have been coming out lately.
Youngjin: Do you watch music shows often?
Soyeon: Sometimes I do, but I tend to mainly watch things on the Internet.
Youngjin: I like to watch variety shows. But last Sunday I fought with my little brother because of one.
Soyeon: Why?

Youngjin: Well, he likes sports and my show came on at the same time as his soccer game. So I just changed the channel while he was in the middle of watching the game.

Soyeon: How can you fight over something like that.

NARRATION *The Hobbies of Modern People*

Modern people have diverse hobbies. Some read, and some enjoy music or movies. There are people who like photography, and those who exercise hard. There are some that make time to travel or go hiking. Some people who do office work even learn cooking or foreign languages after work. Also, people gain new information and meet various others through online communities.

Modern life may be busy, but it's important for us to make time to do the things we like, because we can relieve stress and experience new things while doing what we enjoy.

CULTURE *Ssireum (Korean Wrestling)*

Ssireum is Korea's traditional wrestling that can be dated back to over one thousand years ago. On Dano Day, the fifth day of the fifth month on the lunar calendar, among the many festivities, there was always a ssireum competition held. The winner of the competition was given the title, "Cheonhajangsa," meaning "The Strongest Human in the World," and would receive an ox as a prize. Nowadays, ssireum has become a national sport, and is frequently broadcast on television. Ssireum matches start with both athletes sitting in a sandpit and grasping each other's satba. The satba is a long piece of cloth that is wrapped around the waist and right thigh. Points are obtained by making the opponent touch the sand with any part of their body other than their feet.

11과 한국의 명절

Lesson 11 Holidays in Korea

Conversation 1 새해 복 많이 받으세요.

Conversation 1

수빈, 수진: 아버지, 어머니 새해 복 많이 받으세요.
아버지: 그래, 너희들도 모두 새해 복 많이 받고 건강해라.
어머니: 수빈이는 원하는 직장에 들어가고 수진이는
대학 시험에 합격해라.
수진: 아버지, 어머니께서도 올해 건강하세요.
아버지: 그래, 고맙다. 자, 여기 세뱃돈 받아.
수빈, 수진: 감사합니다.

마크가 수빈이네 집에 떡국을 먹으러 왔다.

마크: 어머니, 떡국이 정말 맛있어요.
어머니: 맛있게 먹어줘서 고마워요.
한국 음식을 좋아하나 봐요.[G11.1]
마크: 네, 떡국은 처음인데 너무 맛있어서
두 그릇이나 먹었어요.
어머니 우리 집에 자주 놀러 와요. 또 끓여 줄게요.
마크: 네, 고맙습니다.
수빈: 마크 씨, 윷놀이 할 줄 알아요?
마크: 방송에서 보기는 봤는데[G11.2] 아직 못 해 봤어요.
수빈: 그럼, 오늘 같이 한번 해 봐요.

COMPREHENSION QUESTIONS

1. 수빈이와 수진이는 설날 무엇을 했습니까?
2. 수빈이와 수진이가 새해에 원하는 것이 무엇입니까?
3. 마크는 왜 수빈이네 집에 왔습니까?
4. 수빈이와 마크는 식사 후에 무엇을 하기로 했습니까?

NEW WORDS

NOUN

그릇	bowl, plate
놀이공원	amusement park
떡국	rice cake soup
명절	traditional holidays
민속촌	Folk Village
방송	broadcasting, television
복	blessing
새해	New Year
설날	New Year's Day
세배	New Year's bow
세뱃돈	New Year's cash gift
윷놀이	yut game
입시	(college) entrance exam
차례	ancestral rites
친척	relatives
표정	(facial) expression
합격(하다)	pass, acceptance

VERB

놀러 가다	to go on an outing
놀러 오다	to come around
들어가다	to get (a job/work)
원하다	to want, wish
지내다	to have (a ceremony)

ADVERB

또	again
제대로	properly

ADJECTIVE

밝다	be bright

INTERJECTION

아이고	oh my

SUFFIX

~(으)ㄴ가 보다/나 보다	It seems/I guess
~기는 ~하다	did . . . , but

NEW EXPRESSIONS

1. 명절: Korean traditional holidays are called 명절 while other holidays with legal or political significance (Memorial Day, Liberation Day, etc.) are generally called 공휴일/국경일.

2. 세배: On special occasions, Koreans bow to their elders, starting in the standing position and ending in the prostrate position on the floor. A New Year's bow is called 세배 while the traditional bow for other occasions is called 큰절 (*lit.* 'a big bow').

3. V.S. ~어라/아라
This ending is the imperative form of the plain style (-다 form) and is often used to address children, younger siblings, and grandchildren. Parents often use this form with their children. Between close friends, both the plain style and the intimate style can be used.

Plain	지금 가라	밥 먹어라	앉아라
Intimate	지금 가	밥 먹어	앉아

4. 새해 복 많이 받으세요.
This expression is used when you make a big New Year's bow to elders. Literally it means, "Please receive many blessings in the New Year." It is equivalent to "Happy New Year."

5. 시험에 합격하다/불합격하다
The verb 합격하다 ('to pass') takes a noun with the particle 에. 시험에 불합격하다 ('to fail an exam') is synonymous with 시험에 떨어지다. Some words take the negative prefix 불.

친절	kindness	불친절	unkindness
합격	passing	불합격	failure
편하다	to be comfortable	불편하다	to be uncomfortable
	to be convenient		to be inconvenient

Grammar

G11.1 V.S.~나 보다/A.S.~(으)ㄴ가 보다 'It seems/I guess'

Examples

(1) A: 한국에 온 지 얼마나 됐어요? 한국말을 잘 하시네요.
B: 작년 8월에 왔으니까 한 일 년쯤 됐**나 봐요**.

(2) 민지:	마크 씨, 좋은 일이 있**나 봐요**? 표정이 밝아요.	Mark, I guess things are going well with you. You look cheerful.
마크:	네, 원하던 직장에 들어갔어요.	Yes, I've got my dream job.
(3)	마크가 오늘은 기분이 안 좋**은가 봐요**. 얼굴이 어두워요.	It looks like Mark is not in a good mood today. He has a gloomy look.

(4) 민지가 하루 종일 전화를 안 받아요. 많이 바**쁜가 봐요**.

Notes

1. Presumption vs. inference

Recall that ~(으)ㄹ 거예요 expresses the speaker's presumption about an event that is not directly accessible on the part of the speaker. The presumption may be made out of sheer conjecture without any evidence at hand. For example,

(i) A: 이번 봄방학 때 뭐 할 거예요?
B: 놀이공원에 갈 거예요.

(ii) 린다: 샌디 요즘 뭐 해요?
마크: 아마 한국 갔을 거예요.

On the other hand, some situations are conjectured, not by presumption, but based on some kind of evidence; that is, one may indicate that he or she draws a conclusion or makes a judgment, upon hearing or seeing something. In this case, it is an inferential judgment that the speaker is making.

Two kinds of inferential processes

There are two expressions in Korean to indicate that something is an inferential judgment based on some evidence; they are ~나 봐요/~(으)ㄴ가 봐요 and ~겠, depending on the kind of inferential process involved.

Recall that ~겠 indicates that the conveyed message is a conjecture based on evidence. For example,

A: 오늘 늦잠을 잤어요.
B: 수업에 늦었겠어요.

In this example, B's inference that A must have been late for class is based on A's saying that he got up late today. This is a deductive reasoning process involved with ~겠 where a consequence is inferred based on the speaker's knowledge of its source and a general rule. More examples of deductive reasoning expressed with ~겠:

[구름이 끼면 보통 비가 와요.]
구름이 끼었어요. → 비가 오겠어요.
[숙제가 많으면 힘들어요.]
A: 한국어 201은 숙제가 매일 있어요.
B: 와, 힘들겠어요.

With ~나 봐요/~(으)ㄴ가 봐요 'it seems, it looks like, I guess', a different kind of inferential process, namely abductive reasoning, is involved; that is, given a situation, one can infer a possible source or cause of the given situation. In (1), for example, in responding to A's question, B's answer provides information with regard to the length of his stay in Korea. In (2), Mark's feeling good (cause/source) is inferred from his cheerful look (consequence). Similarly, in (3), Mark's not feeling good is inferred from his gloomy look. In (4), 민지 being busy is inferred from her not answering the phone.

2. ~나 봐요 is used for verbs, and ~(으)ㄴ가 봐요/~(이)ㄴ가 봐요 is used for adjectives and the copula 이다, respectively. With ~었, however, ~나 봐요 is used for verbs, adjectives, and the copula.

	Plain	**With ~었**
Verbs	~나 봐요	~었나 봐요
Adjectives	~(으)ㄴ가 봐요	~었나 봐요
Copula	~(이)ㄴ가 봐요	~이었나/였나 봐요

Exercises

Complete the dialogue by providing a statement of inferential judgment, using either ~겠 or ~나/~(으)ㄴ가 봐(요).

(1) (i) A: 날씨가 별로 안 좋네요.

B: 네, 구름이 많이 낀 걸 보니까 비가 오겠어요.

(ii) A: 저 이번 학기에 전부 A 받았어요.

B: 공부를 열심히 했나 봐요.

(2) A: 저 다음 주에 한국에 가요.

B: 그래요? ________________________________.

A: 오랫동안 친척들을 못 만났거든요.

(3) A: 아이고, 졸려!

B: ____.

(4) A: (Seeing B wearing short sleeves in cold weather)

________________________________. 자켓 안 가져 오셨어요?

B: 네, 아침에 나올 때는 괜찮았는데 갑자기 추워졌네요.

(5) A: 제니가 요즘 안 보여요.

B: 글쎄요. 요즘 대학 입시 준비하고 있던데,

__________________.

Grammar

G11.2 ~기는 . . . ~다/하다 'did . . . , but'

Examples

(1) 소연: 민속촌 구경 안 가실래요?
설연휴 동안 행사가 많거든요.
유진: 와, 그거 재미있겠네요.
저도 듣**기는 들었는데/했는데** 아직 못 가 봤거든요.

(2) A: 밤 1시가 넘었는데 안 자요? — It's past 1 a.m.; aren't you sleeping?
B: 자**기는 자야/해야 하는데** 내일 시험이 있어서 공부해야 돼요. — As for sleeping I do have to sleep, but I have a test tomorrow so I have to study.

(3) A: 요새 한국어 배우세요?
B 배우**기는 배우는데/하는데** 제대로 못해요.
근데 어렵**기는 어려운데/한데** 재미있어요.

(4) A: 어제 잘 잤어요?
B: 자**기는 잘 잤어요**/잘 자**기는 했어요**. 그런데 아직도 졸려요.

Notes

1. Recall that ~기 is a nominalizer that makes a predicate a noun. For example, 듣기 means 'hearing'. The topic marker 는 selects an item and makes it a topic or subject matter of conversation. Combined together, ~기는 ~다 is used when the speaker picks up an idea that has just been entertained and acknowledges its partial validity, but advances a rather different idea or value.

The difference between 들었어요 and 듣기는 했어요 is that the former simply means 'I heard (it)', whereas the latter means 'As for hearing, I did hear, but . . .' or 'Hearing, I did but . . .'

2. This pattern is typically combined with ~는데 (rather than a simple sentence ender such as 해요), as in (1)–(3) to signal that what is actually true is not quite the same as what has been said.

3. After ~기는, the same verb may be repeated, as in 듣기는 들었는데, or 하다 'to do' may substitute for the second verb, e.g., 듣기는 했는데.

Exercises

Using ~기는 하다, construct a dialogue that acknowledges what the other person has said and yet contrasts it.

(1) A: 어제 잘 잤어요?
B: 자기는 잘 잤는데, 아직도 졸려요.

(2) A: 테니스 잘 쳐요?
B: ______________________.

(3) A: 한국어 재미있어요?
B: ______________________.

(4) A: 컴퓨터 샀어요?
B: ______________________.

(5) A: 설 잘 보내셨어요?
B: ______________________.

Conversation 2 추석에는 어떤 음식을 먹어요?

스티브가 처음으로 한국에서 추석을 지내게 되었다.

Conversation 2

스티브: 소연 씨는 추석에 보통 뭐 해요?

소연: 아침에는 차례를 지내고 오후에는 가족들하고 시간을 보내거나[G11.3] 친구들을 만나요.

스티브: 차례가 뭐예요?

소연: 음식을 차려 놓고 조상들께 감사 드리는 거예요. 그런데 요즘엔 차례를 안 지내는 집이 많대요.[G11.4]

스티브: 아, 네. 그런데 추석에는 어떤 음식을 먹어요?

소연: 보통 송편을 먹어요.

스티브: 아, 저도 한번 먹어 본 적이 있는 것 같아요. 반달처럼 생긴 떡 말이지요?

소연: 네, 맞아요.
참, 스티브 씨, 추석 연휴 동안 민속촌에서 행사가 많은데 내일 구경하러 갈래요?

스티브: 아, 네. 그거 재미있겠네요!
근데 아침에는 일이 좀 있고, 오후라면[G11.5] 괜찮아요.

소연: 그럼, 몇 시쯤이 좋으세요?

스티브: 오후에는 아무 때나 좋아요.

COMPREHENSION QUESTIONS

1. 소연이는 추석에 보통 무엇을 합니까?
2. 차례는 무엇입니까?
3. 소연이와 스티브는 추석 연휴에 무엇을 하기로 했습니까?

NEW WORDS

NOUN	
떡	rice cake
반달	half moon
법대	law school
소식	news
송편	*songpyen*
어린이	child
연휴	long weekend
영업	business
의대	medical school
전국	the whole nation
조상	ancestor
추석	Korean Thanksgiving
추수	harvest
행사	event, function

ADJECTIVE	
한산하다	be inactive, slack

VERB	
벗어나다	get out of
붐비다	be crowded
생기다	to look like
앞두다	to have something ahead
차다	be full

ADVERB	
꽉	tightly, fully
대부분	mostly
절대	never

PRONOUN	
아무	any

PARTICLE	
처럼	like, as

SUFFIX	
~(이)라면	if it were
~거나	or
~대요/래요	hearsay

NEW EXPRESSIONS

1. 추석을 보내다: 추석 (Chuseok) is celebrated. 보내다 means 'to send, spend, pass (time)'.

2. 차례 is a Confucian memorial service held on New Year's Day (설날) and Chuseok (추석). The memorial service held on the anniversary of an ancestor's death is called 제사, which is often performed at night, while 차례 is performed in the morning. The verb 지내다 is used with these nouns (차례, 제사).

3. 송편 is a kind of rice cake in the shape of a half moon. The inside of 송편 is filled with chestnuts, beans, or sesame seeds. 송편 is steamed with pine needles so that the pieces don't stick to each other and that the fragrance of pine needles can be tasted.

Grammar

G11.3 ~거나 'V1 or V2'

Examples

(1) 소연: 민호 씨는 시간 있을 때 주로 뭐 하세요?
민호: 집에서 비디오 보**거나** 친구하고 영화 보러 가요. 소연 씨는요? — I watch videos at home or go to the movies.
소연: 저는 신문이나 소설 책을 읽어요.

(2) 성희: 점심 보통 어디서 먹어요?
소연: 학교 식당에서 먹**거나** 기숙사 식당에 가서 먹어요. — I eat at the school cafeteria or I go to the dorm cafeteria and eat.
성희 씨는요?
성희: 저는 학교 식당이나 집에 가서 먹어요.

(3) 소연: 성희 씨는 왜 아직 안 와요?
유진: 아직 자고 있**거나** 늦게 나와서 버스를 놓쳤을 거예요.
(버스를 놓치다 'to miss the bus')

(4) 몸이 아프**거나** 피곤할 때는 일찍 자는 게 제일 좋아요.

Notes

1. ~거나 is attached to a verb or adjective stem to indicate a disjunctive choice; that is, in A~거나 B, at least one of the situations, A or B, is true, like 'or' in English.

2. ~(이)나 is attached to a noun, as in (1) and (2).

Exercises

Answer the given questions, using ~거나 or ~(이)나.

(1) 소연: 중요한 인터뷰를 앞두고 주로 뭐 하세요?
민호: 집에서 책을 읽거나 뉴스를 봐요.

(2) A: 저녁에 보통 뭐 하세요?
B: ________________________________.

(3) A: 소연 씨 어디 있어요?
B: ________________________________.

(4) A: 감기 걸렸을 때 어떻게 하세요?
B: ________________________________.

(5) A: 점심 보통 어디서 드세요?
B: ________________________________.

G11.4 Expressing hearsay: ~대요/(이)래요.

Examples

(1) A: 하숙집을 옮겨야겠어요.
B: 왜요? 지금 사시는 아파트가 불편하세요?
A: 아니요, 깨끗하고 다 좋은데, 집주인이 다음 달부터 방값을 올**린대요**. — No, it's clean and nice, but my landlady says she's raising the rent from next month.

(2) A: 학교 앞 하숙집들 괜찮아요?
B: 내 친구가 학교 법대 앞에서 하숙하는데, 하숙비도 싸고 괜찮**대요**. — One of my friends is living at a boardinghouse in front of the law school. She says that the rent is low and it's okay.

(3) 민지: 린다 씨, 샌디 소식 들었어요? 한국 갔**대요**.
린다: 그래요? 언제 갔**대요**?
민지: 지난주에 갔**대요**. 가서 스티브도 만**난대요**.

(4) A: 저 사람 누구예요?
B: 샌디 동생**이래요**.

Notes

1. ~대요 is used when the information conveyed is not from the speaker's firsthand knowledge, but something he or she has heard from somebody else.

2. ~대요 is a contracted form of the more general quotation construction ~다고 해요, which consists of the plain-style ending ~다 plus 고해요 'say that . . .' where 고 is a quotative particle: ~다 + 고 해요 = ~대요.

3. With the copula ~이, ~다 changes into ~라 when it occurs in a quotation such that ~래 is used instead of ~대; that is,

N~이래요 (after a consonant): 저 애 샌디 동생이래요.
N~래요 (after a vowel): 저 사람 샌디 오빠래요.

4. 대요/래요 shows the same temporal marking as the plain style; that is, verbs take ~는/ㄴ (~는 after a consonant, ~ㄴ after a vowel) for non-past tense, whereas adjectives do not take any temporal marking.

Variation between verbs and adjectives in temporal marking:

	Plain style		**Hearsay**	
	Non-past	Past	Non-past	Past
Verb	~는다/ㄴ다	~었/았다	~는/ㄴ대요	~었/았대요
Adjective	~다	~었/았다	~대요	~었/았대요
Copula	(이)다	이었다/였다	(이)래요	이었대요/였대요

Exercises

1. Practice as in the example.

(1) 샌디가 의대에 가요.
→ 샌디가 의대에 간대요.

(2) 학생들이 아침을 안 먹어요.

(3) 이번 주는 날씨가 좋아요.

(4) 학교 도서관은 늘 붐비지만 주말에는 한산해요.

(5) 명절에는 식당들이 대부분 영업을 안 해요.

(6) 마크는 한국에 온 지 반 년 됐어요.

2. Complete the dialogue using the hearsay form.

(1) 린다: 마크 씨, 샌디 한국에 언제 가요?
마크: 다음 주에 간대요.

(2) A: 학교 앞 미용실 어때요?
B: ______________. 항상 붐비더라고요.

(3) A: 괜찮은 식당 좀 알아요?
B: 학교 건너편에 하나 있는데 한식 전문______________.

(4) A: 저 사람 누구예요?
B: ______________________________.
A: 샌디한테 오빠가 있었어요?
B: 얼마 전에 홍콩에서 ______________________________.

(5) A: 샌디는 참 건강하네요.
B: ______________________________.
A: 나도 매일 한 시간씩 걸어야겠어요.

(6) 린다: 샌디한테서 연락 왔어요?
마크: 네, 어제 전화 왔는데, ______________________________.
린다: 뭐가 그렇게 재미있대요?
마크: 서울을 벗어나 전국을 여행하는 게 너무 즐겁대요.
내일은 경주로 ______________.

G11.5 N~(이)라면 'If it were/is'

Examples

(1) 소연: 이번 토요일 3시에 예약하고 싶은데요.
직원: 토요일은 예약이 꽉 찼는데요. 일요일**이라면** 괜찮은데요.

(2)	A:	저 사람 혹시 스티브 누나 아니에요?	Is that person Steve's older sister by any chance?
	B:	가서 한 번 알아 볼까요?	Shall I go over there and find out?
	A:	스티브 누나**라면** 스티브 소식 좀 물어보세요.	If she is Steve's older sister, ask her about Steve.

(3) A: 나는 배우가 되고 싶은데, 아버지는 의사가 되라고 하셔서 어떻게 해야 할지 모르겠어. 너**라면** 어떻게 할래?
B: 나는 내가 하고 싶은 일을 할 거야.

Notes

N~(이)라면 is used when the identity of an entity is hypothesized, and is best translated as 'If it were/is' or 'If you mean to say N'.

Exercises

Using 내가 만일 ~(이)라면, say what you would like to do if you were the given item.

(1) [부자] <u>내가 만일 부자라면 집을 사고 싶어요</u>.
(2) [빌 게이츠]
(3) [선생님]
(4) [대통령]
(5) [슈퍼맨]

Narration 민족[1] 대이동[2]

명절이 되면 전국의 고속도로는 가족들을 만나기 위해 고향으로 가는 차들로 붐빈다. 특히 서울에서 고향으로 가는 사람들이 많다. 복잡한 교통을 피하려고 새벽에 떠나기도 한다. 고속도로는 차들로 붐비지만 오랜만에 부모님도 뵙고 가족들과 즐거운 시간을 보낼 수 있기 때문에 고향으로 떠나는 사람들의 표정은 무척 밝다.

대부분의 가게들은 명절 연휴 동안 문을 닫는다. 그래서 많은 사람들이 떠나 버린 서울 거리는 한산하다. 그렇지만 박물관이나 놀이공원은 연휴 동안 여러 가지 행사를 한다. 극장도 오랜만에 시간을 내서 영화를 보러 오는 사람들로 꽉 찬다.

1. 민족: national
2. 대이동: mass migration

COMPREHENSION QUESTIONS

1. 명절이 되면 왜 고속도로가 붐빕니까?
2. 사람들은 왜 고향으로 떠납니까?
3. 명절 연휴 동안 서울은 어떻습니까?
4. 민족 대이동이란 무엇입니까?

NEW EXPRESSIONS

1. 한산하다: 'to be inactive, slack'

시장이 한산하다	The market is not active (with not many people).

Notes

CULTURE

떡국 Tteokguk

모든 명절에는 그 날을 위한[1] 별미[2]를 준비하는데, 설에는 떡국을 먹는다[3]. 떡국은 동전 모양[4]의 떡을 소고기[5] 국물[6]에 넣어 끓인 음식이다. 흔히[7] '우리 나이'라고 부르는 한국 나이는 태어나는 순간[8]부터 시작된다. 즉[9], 아기가 태어나는 순간 한 살이 되고, 설이 되면 또 한 살을 더 먹는다.

서양식[10] 나이를 사용해야 하는 특별한 상황[11]이 아니면, 사람들은 보통 한국식 나이를 사용한다. 이렇게 설날을 기준[12]으로 나이가 변하기[13] 때문에 "떡국[14] 몇 그릇[15] 먹었어요?"라는 질문이 "올해 몇 살 되었어요?"라는 의미[16]를 갖게 되었다.

1. 위한: for, in order to
2. 별미: gourmet
3. (나이를) 먹다: to age
4. 모양: shape
5. 소고기: beef
6. 국물: soup, broth
7. 흔히: commonly
8. 순간: the moment
9. 즉: that is
10. 서양식: Western style
11. 상황: situation
12. 기준: standard
13. 변하다: to change
14. 떡국: rice cake soup
15. 그릇: bowl
16. 의미: meaning

USAGE

1 *Talking about holidays*

In pairs, practice the following conversations.

(1) 새해 인사

A: 새해 복 많이 받으세요.

B: 네. 새해 복 많이 받으세요.
설날 어떻게 지내셨어요?

A: 부모님께 세배 드리고 식구들이랑 떡국 먹고 윷놀이 했어요.

B: 재미있었겠네요.

(2) 추석

A: 어디 다녀 오세요?

B: 네, 시장에 갔다 오는 길인데 너무 복잡해서
제대로 걷지도 못 했어요.

A: 내일이 추석이라 그래요.
다들 차례도 지내야 하고 가족들이 다 모이니까
음식도 많이 하거든요.

Greetings for Holidays

a. New Year's greeting (새해 인사)
새해 복 많이 받으세요.
올해도 건강하세요.
설날 어떻게 지내셨어요?

b. 추석 인사
추석 잘 보내세요.
추석 잘 보내셨어요?

Exercise 1

Interview your partner with the following questions and report the result to the class.

(1) 지난 설날을 누구하고 어디서 어떻게 보내셨어요?

(2) 작년 추수 감사절에는 뭐 하셨어요?

(3) 제일 기억에 남는 추수감사절/설날이 언제예요?
왜 기억에 남아요?

(4) 봄방학 (spring break) 때 보통 뭐 하세요?

(5) 제일 좋아하는 명절이 뭐예요? 왜요?

Exercise 2

Role play

(1) You are talking with a Korean friend in Busan, Korea. Your friend plans to study in the United States and wants to get information about special holidays that Americans celebrate. Describe to your friend in Korean about New Year's celebrations, 4th of July, and Thanksgiving.
(July 4th 미국 독립기념일)

(2) It is your first Thanksgiving after starting college. You go home for the holiday and your parents ask you about how your classes are, if you are dating anyone, and what it's like at school.

Exercise 3

Compare the following holidays and report any similarities and/or differences between the ways Koreans and Americans celebrate them.

(1) 설날 vs. New Year's Day in the United States

(2) 추석 vs. Thanksgiving

2 *Making suggestions and arranging schedules*

Practice the following conversation.

(1) Plan for New Year's break

소연: 이번 연휴에 민속촌 구경 안 가실래요?
설 연휴 동안 행사가 많거든요.
유진: 저도 민속촌에 대해서 듣기는 들었는데 아직 못 가 봤어요.
그럼 내일 오후 어떠세요?
소연: 내일 오후라면 괜찮은데요. 몇 시에 만날까요?
유진: 저는 오후에는 아무 때나 좋아요.
소연: 그럼 1시에 민속촌 앞에서 만나는 게 어때요?

(2) Plan for Thanksgiving

영미: 이번 추수감사절에 뭐 하실 거예요?
샌디: 별 계획이 없어요.
영미: 그럼 우리 부모님 집에 같이 안 갈래요?
부모님도 샌디 씨를 만나고 싶어하시거든요.
샌디: 저도 한번 뵙고 싶은데요. 부모님 댁이 어디세요?
영미: 내 차로 같이 운전해서 가면 어떨까요?
샌디: 좋지요. 초대해 주셔서 고맙습니다.

Exercise 1

Practice the above conversation with each of the following topics:

(1) You plan to go to Las Vegas during a spring break with your friend. Call your friend to make arrangements for the trip.

(2) You want to invite a friend for a Thanksgiving dinner at your place.

(3) You want to have a barbecue party at a park on July 4th. Call and invite a friend. Make arrangements regarding location, time, activities, and food.

(4) You want to go on a ski trip during Christmas break with your friend. Call and ask him/her to go to a ski resort in Colorado. Make a plan together.

(5) You want to take a vacation with your friend during Labor Day weekend. You have not decided on a destination yet. Call and talk with a travel agent to plan the trip.

Exercise 2

Imagine that your Korean pen pal is visiting your city during a Christmas–New Year's vacation. Your friend has a limited budget and wants to know more about your town. Call your pen pal and make suggestions. Arrange at least one special event for him/her.

3 *Reading newspaper articles*

Read the following newspaper article and answer the questions.

옛날이 살아있는 민속관 나들이

설날을 설날답게 즐기려면 민속관이 적당하다. 민속관은 단순한 박물관이 아니다. 인형, 사진 등을 이용해 전통 민속 환경을 실감나게 연출하는 교육 장소이다. 민속은 어른들에게는 향수를 주고 어린이들에게는 호기심을 준다. 옛것이 새것처럼 살아있는 곳이 바로 민속관이다.

대부분의 민속관은 입장료가 싸고 도시 근교에 위치해 교통도 밀리지 않는다. 국립 민속박물관이나 서울 롯데월드 민속관은 할아버지에서 손자까지 설날 가족 나들이에 적당한 곳이다.

국립 민속박물관: 설날 장사를 가장 못하는 곳 중에 하나다. 한복 차림의 입장객은 입장료가 무료이기 때문이다. 오천여 점의 유물을 볼 수 있다. '국립'이기 때문에 아무래도 재미보다 고상하고 잔잔한 분위기이다. 박물관 앞 광장에는 연날리기, 줄넘기 등 민속놀이 기구도 준비되어 있다.

한국 민속촌 민속관: 용인 민속촌 내에 지난 해 12월에 새로 문을 열었다. 이곳에서는 조선 후기 한 가족의 명절 풍습을 보여준다.

롯데월드 민속박물관: 박물관이면서도 매직 비전, 멀티 비전 등이 있는 민속테마파크. 재미있고 구경거리가 많다. 오후 11시까지 야간 개장.

New words

옛날	old days	나들이	going out
적당하다	to be suitable	단순한	simple
인형	a doll, a puppet	이용하다	to utilize
전통	tradition	환경	environment
연출하다	to show, to stage	교육	education
향수	homesick	호기심	curiosity
근교	the suburbs	위치	a location
장사	business	무료	free of charge
오천여점	about 5,000 pieces	유물	relics
고상하다	to be elegant	잔잔한	calm
광장	a plaza	연날리기	kite flying
줄넘기	jumping rope	기구	tools
주제	a theme	조선시대	Joseon dynasty
후기	later days	풍습	customs
야간	night	개장	opening
휴장	closing		

Exercise 1

Mark T (true) or F (false) for the following statements.

(1) _______ Most folk museums are located far from the city.

(2) _______ The admission fee to the folk museums is inexpensive.

(3) _______ Lotte Folk Museum is open until late evening.

(4) _______ All three museums are open during the New Year's holiday season.

Exercise 2

Answer the following questions in Korean.

(1) 국립민속박물관이 설날에 돈을 벌지 못하는 이유는 무엇입니까?
(2) 가장 최근에 문을 연 민속관은 어디 있습니까?
(3) 입장료가 가장 싼 민속관의 이름은 무엇입니까?
(4) 민속박물관이 설날 가족 나들이에 좋은 이유는 무엇입니까?

Notes

Lesson 11. Holidays in Korea

CONVERSATION 1 *Happy New Year*

After the ancestral rites on New Year's Day, Soobin and Sujin give the New Year's bow to their parents.

Soobin, Sujin: Happy New Year, Mom and Dad!
Father: Hey, Happy New Year to you too kids, and be healthy this year.
Mother: Soobin, I hope you get the job you want, and Sujin, I hope you pass your university entrance exam.
Sujin: I hope you guys stay healthy too, Mom and Dad.
Father: Alright, thanks. Here, take your New Year's money.
Soobin, Sujin: Thank you.

Mark came to Soobin's to eat rice cake soup.

Mark: This rice cake soup is really tasty.
Mother: Thank you for eating so well. You must like Korean food.
Mark: Yes, it's my first time trying tteokguk, but it's so good I had two bowls.
Mother: You should come visit our house more often. I'll make it for you again.
Mark: Yes, I will. Thank you.
Soobin: Mark, do you know how to play yut?
Mark: I saw it on TV, but I haven't tried it yet.
Soobin: Then let's try it together today.

CONVERSATION 2 *What Do You Eat on Chuseok?*

Steve is celebrating his first Chuseok.

Steve: Soyeon, what do you normally do on Chuseok?
Soyeon: In the morning I do ancestral rites, and in the afternoon, I either spend time with my family or see friends.
Steve: What are ancestral rites?
Soyeon: It's where we prepare food to show appreciation to our ancestors. But I heard nowadays there are many families who don't perform ancestral rites.
Steve: Oh, I see. By the way, what do you eat on Chuseok?
Soyeon: I normally eat songpyeon.

Steve: I think I've tried that once. It's the rice cakes that looks like a half moon, right?

Soyeon: Yep, that's right. Oh, Steve, during this Chuseok weekend, there are going to be a lot of events going on at folk villages. Do you want to go check them out with me tomorrow?

Steve: Yeah, that sounds like fun! But I do have something going on tomorrow morning, I'm good if it's in the afternoon though.

Soyeon: Then what time will be good for you?

Steve: Any time in the afternoon is fine.

NARRATION *Holiday Traffic*

On the holidays, all highways in Korea are packed with people driving to their hometowns to see their families. There are especially many people leaving from Seoul to go to their hometowns. There are even people who leave at dawn in hopes of avoiding the traffic. While the highways may be packed with cars, people's faces are bright with excitement to see their parents for the first time in a long while, and the prospect of enjoying spending time with their families.

Most stores close during the holiday weekends, so the streets in Seoul become quiet after many people have left. However, museums and amusement parks hold various events over the holiday weekend. Theaters are also crowded with people who finally got the chance to make time to watch movies.

CULTURE *Tteokguk*

There are special, unique delicacies that are prepared for each holiday, and on Seol, it's tteokguk. Tteokguk is a dish that contains coin-shaped tteok that was boiled in beef broth. Korean age, which is commonly called "our age," begins the moment someone is born. That is, a child that was just born is one year old, and gains a year on each Seol.

Outside of special circumstances where Western age needs to be used, people normally use Korean age. Because Seollal is the standard for when age changes, the question "how many bowls of tteokguk have you eaten?" carries the same meaning as, "how old are you turning this year?"

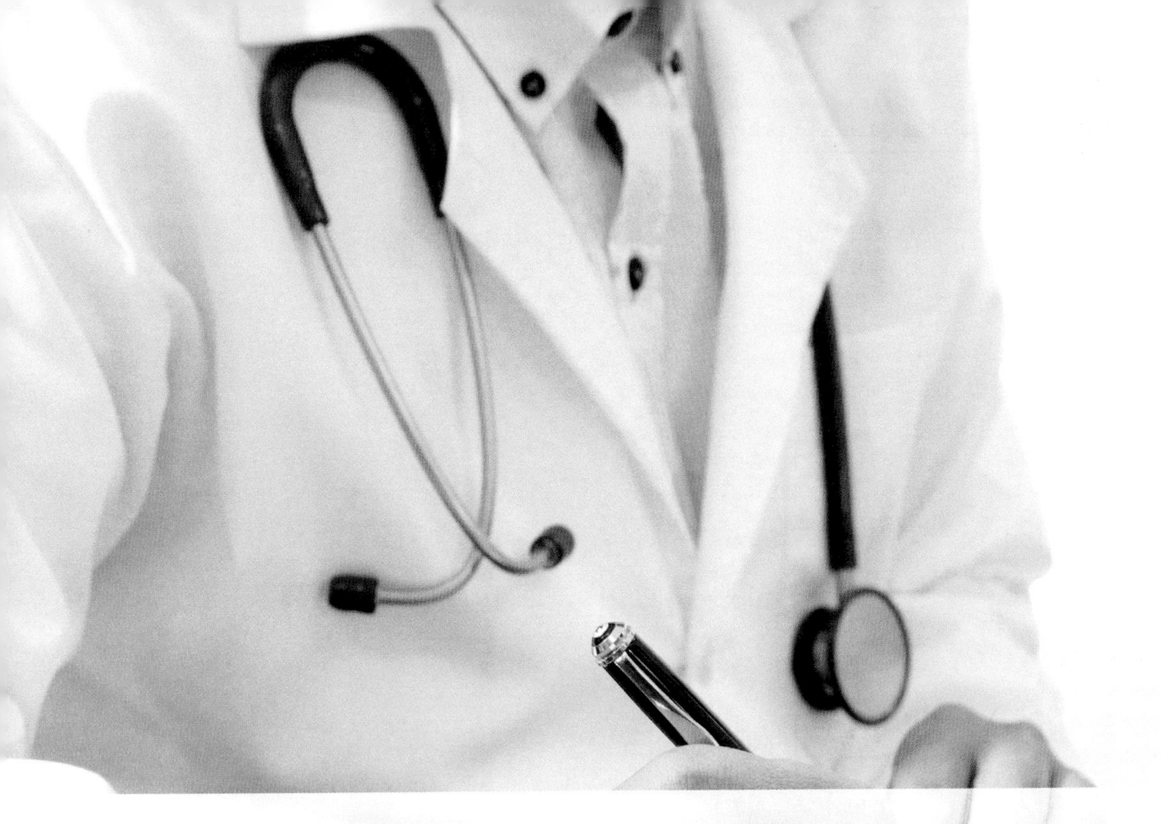

12과 병원과 약국

Lesson 12 Hospitals and Drugstores

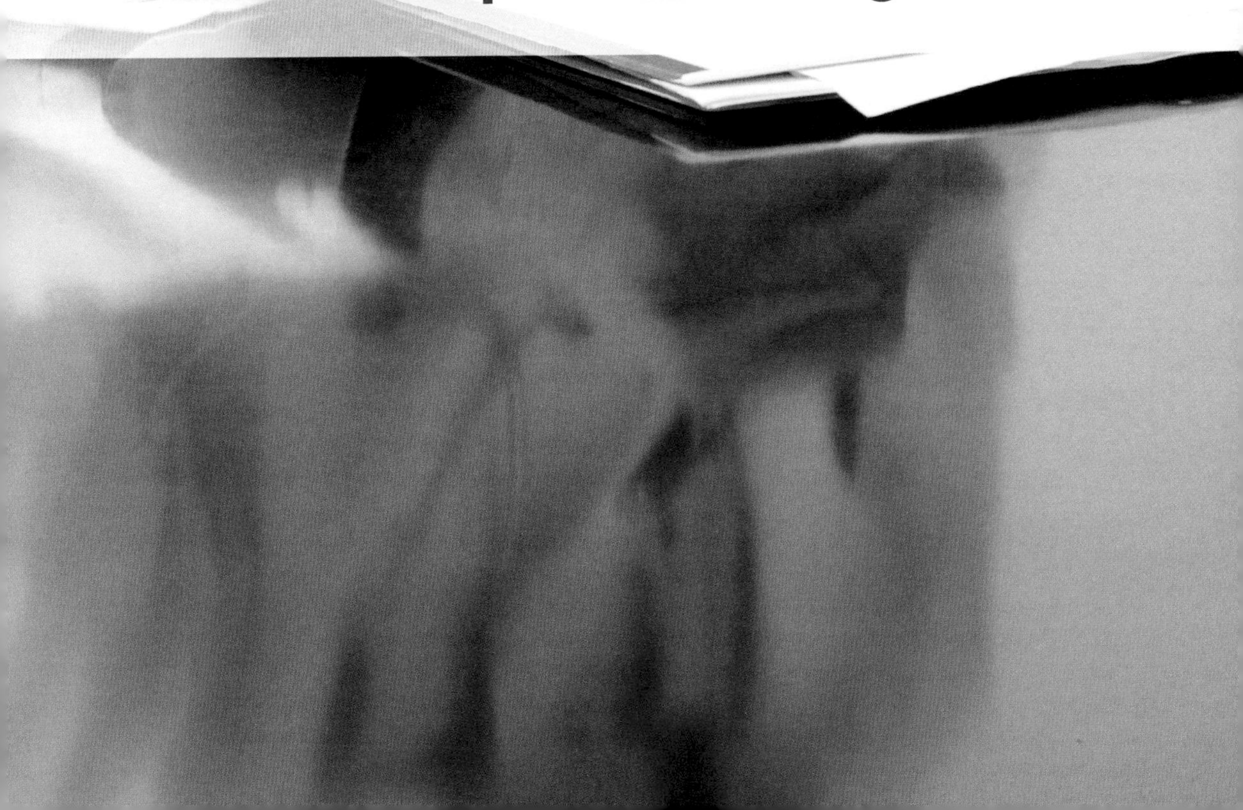

Conversation 1 어디가 불편하세요?

민지는 몸이 아파서 병원에 갔다.

Conversation 1

의사: 어디가 불편하세요?

민지: 열도 좀 있고 기침을 심하게 해요.
너무 아파서 아무것도 못 먹었어요.

의사: 또 다른 증상은 없나요?[G12.1]

민지: 3일 전부터 소화도 안 되고 그랬어요.

의사: 한번 봅시다.

진찰을 한다.

민지: 많이 안 좋은가요?[G12.1]

의사: 심한 독감에 걸리셨네요. 기침을 너무 많이
해서 목이 많이 상했어요.

민지: 좀 더 일찍 올 걸 그랬네요.[G12.2]

의사: 우선 이틀 치 약을 처방해 드릴 테니까
약 드시고 푹 쉬세요.

민지: 네, 알겠습니다.

잠시 후 병원 근처 약국에서

의사: 약 여기 있습니다. 식후에 한 알씩 하루에 세 번 드세요. 시간 지켜서 드셔야 돼요.

민지: 이 약을 먹으면 졸릴까요?

약사 아니요, 괜찮으실 거예요.

COMPREHENSION QUESTIONS

1. 민지는 어떤 증상 때문에 병원에 갔습니까?
2. 민지는 어디가 아픕니까?
3. 의사는 민지에게 어떤 처방을 했습니까?
4. 약사는 민지에게 무엇이라고 말했습니까?

NEW WORDS

NOUN

기침(하다)	cough
닷새	five days
독감	flu
목	throat
병	disease, illness
병원	hospital
보름	fifteen days
소화	digestion
식후	after a meal
약	medicine
약사	pharmacist
열	fever
열흘	ten days
증상	symptom
진찰(하다)	examination, checkup
처방(하다)	prescription
휴식	rest

VERB

꺼내다	to take out
위하다	to care for
지키다	to protect

ADJECTIVE

불편하다	be uncomfortable
심하다	be severe

ADVERB

따로	separately
푹	deeply, completely

COUNTER

알	pills (counter)
치	amount for . . .

SUFFIX

~(으)ㄹ걸 그랬어요	expressing regret
~(으)ㄴ가요/나요?	Is it (the case) . . .

NEW EXPRESSIONS

1. 어디가 불편하세요? 'Where does it hurt?' is literally 'Where is it uncomfortable?' 불편하다 is more polite than 아프다.

어디가 불편하세요?	속이 답답해요.
	머리가 아파요.
	열이 나요.

2. 한번 봅시다 'Well, let me see' has an authoritative tone.

3. 한 알씩: 씩 'each, respectively, apiece'

이거 얼마씩입니까?
How much are these apiece?

매일 여덟 시간씩 일하면 일주일에 40시간 일하게 돼요.
If we work eight hours a day, we will be working 40 hours a week.

이 약은 어른은 두 알씩, 아이들은 한 알씩 먹어야 합니다.
As for this medicine, adults should take two tablets and children one tablet.

4. 하루에 세 번: 에 'per'

이 사과가 두 개에 1000원이에요.
하루에 밥을 세 번 먹어요.
이 잡지는 일주일에 한 번씩 옵니다.

Grammar

G12.1 AS~(으)ㄴ가요?/ VS~나요? 'Is it (the case), like, . . .'

Examples

(1) [Minji is seeing a doctor.]

민지: 저 며칠 전부터 기침이 나고 열이 나는데, 감기**인가요**?
의사: 한 번 봅시다. 목이 상했네요.
민지: 많이 상했**나요**?
의사: 네, 목 건강을 위해서 열흘이나 보름 동안 찬 음료수는 드시지 마세요.

(2) 민지: 저 민진데요. 동수가 오늘 학교에 안 와서요.
동수 엄마: 아, 동수가 좀 아파요.
민지: 많이 아**픈가요**?
동수 엄마: 감기에 걸려서 열이 좀 심해요.
민지: 네, 그럼 내일도 학교에 못 오**나요**?
동수 엄마: 아마 못 갈 거예요.
민지: 네. 동수한테 몸조리 잘 하라고 전해 주세요.
동수 엄마: 그럴게요.

(3) [Steve is buying a desk.]

스티브: 이 책상 사면 의자도 같이 주**나요**?
점원: 아니요. 의자는 따로 사셔야 돼요.
스티브: 근데 왜 이렇게 비**싼가요**?
점원: 유럽에서 만들었거든요.

Notes

1. ~(으)ㄴ가요/나요? is used in a question by which the speaker indicates his or her uncertainty.

2. It is often used in soliloquy where the speaker asks about the status of someone who he or she is thinking of, as in songs, poetry, or notes of confession.

3. As for the case of ~(으)ㄴ가 봐요/나 봐요 (G11.1), ~(으)ㄴ가요 is attached to an adjective stem and the copula 이~, whereas ~나요 is attached to a verb stem including the verbs of existence 있~ and 없~ and after ~었/았.

~(으)ㄴ가요	~나요
Adjective Stem	Verb/Adjective Stem
copula 이	있/없
	었/았

Exercises

1. Based on the given answers, reconstruct questions by which the speaker indicates his or her uncertainty.

(1) [Steve was absent from school, and Minji heard that Steve is sick. She calls Steve's home and speaks to Steve's roommate.]

민지: 저 민진데요, ________________________?
Roommate: 네, 심한 독감에 걸려서 좀 많이 아파요.
민지: 그럼 내일도 ________________________?
Roommate: 네, 아마 못 갈 거에요.

(2) [Steve asks Minji about homework in the Korean language class because he was absent.]

스티브: ____?
민지: 아니요, 내일까지 내는 숙제는 없어요. 그런데, 모레까지 conversation 1 다 외워야 돼요.

(3) [Yesterday was Michael's birthday. Sophia knows Michael loves to go to a 노래방, and she wonders what happened on his birthday.]

소피아: 마이클 씨, 어제 ________________________?
마이클: 네, 많이 받았어요. 한국어 반 친구들이 선물을 많이 줬어요.
소피아: ____?
마이클: 그럼요. 노래방에서 12시까지 놀았는데요.

2. Thinking of someone you have an affectionate feeling for, write a soliloquy wondering about the status of that person, e.g., what he/she is doing, thinking, or feeling, if he or she is healthy, if there is any serious problems, etc.

Grammar

G12.2 Expressing regret: ~(으)ㄹ걸 (그랬어요)

Examples

(1) 의사: 목이 상하셨군요. 감기에는 휴식이 제일 좋아요.
성희: 네. 조심**할걸 그랬어요**. — I should have been careful (not to catch a cold).

(2) [A and B go to a restaurant and find no table is available]
A: 자리가 없는데요.
B: 예약을 하고 **올걸 그랬어요**. — We should have made a reservation . . .

(3) 성희: 아휴, 배 아파!
민지: 많이 아파? 언제부터 아픈데?
성희: 응, 아까는 별로 안 아파서 그냥 약만 먹었는데, 병원에 **갈걸 그랬나** 봐.

(4) A: 어, 비가 오네! 우산 좀 꺼내 봐요.
B: 우산 안 가져 왔어요.
A: 오늘 일기예보에서 비 온다 그랬잖아요.
B: 우산을 가지고 나**올걸 그랬나** 봐요.
아까 집에서 나올 때는 비가 안 왔거든요.

Notes

1. ~(으)ㄹ걸 expresses a feeling of regret about one's past action by specifying what should have been done instead.

2. After the expression ~(으)ㄹ걸 one may say what he or she actually did as in (1) or just 그랬다 as in (2), which literally means 'did so'; note that it is always in the past tense. In casual conversation 그랬다 can be omitted altogether.

Exercises

Using ~(으)ㄹ걸 그랬어요, express your regret in the context of the given situation.

(1) [식당에 자리가 없어요.]
예약을 하고 올걸 그랬어요.

(2) [시험에서 C밖에 못 받았어요.]
______________________________.

(3) [택시를 타고 가다가 길이 막혀서 늦었어요.]
______________________________.

(4) [백화점에 갔는데 벌써 문을 닫았어요.]
______________________________.

(5) [점심에 뭘 먹을까 하다가 피자를 먹으러 갔는데 맛이 없었어요.]
______________________________.

Notes

CULTURE

서양의학과 한의학 Western Medicine and Oriental Medicine

20세기 한국에 서양의학[1]이 소개되기 전까지는 한의학[2]이라고 하는 전통 의학이 사람들의 질병[3]을 치료하고 건강을 증진시키는[4] 유일한[5] 방법[6]이었다. 한의학에는 보통 한약[7]과 침술[8]이 있는데, 한의학은 오래 전 중국 의학기술[9]을 한국인의 신체특성[10]에 맞도록 발달시킨[11] 것이다.

침술은 몸의 356개의 부분[12] 중 적절한[13] 곳에 침[14]을 놓는 것이다. 그리고 한의사들은 감초[15], 쑥[16], 인삼[17], 녹용[18], 등으로 만든 약재[19]를 처방한다. 한의사들을 길러내는[20] 한의학 대학도 있다. 많은 한국인들이 서양의학에서 부족한[21] 부분을 한의학으로 보충한다[22].

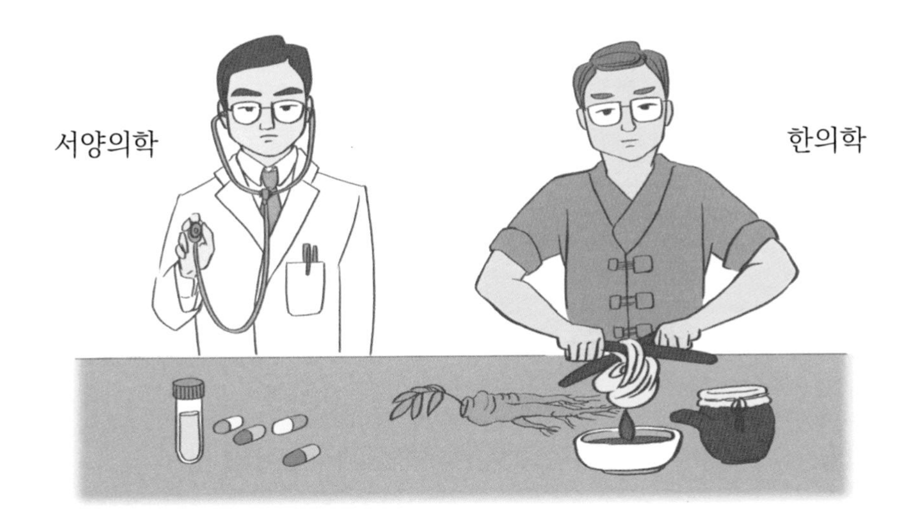

1. 서양의학: Western medicine
2. 한의학: Oriental medicine
3. 질병: illness, disease
4. 증진시키다: to increase
5. 유일한: one and only
6. 방법: method
7. 한약: herbal tonic
8. 침술: acupuncture
9. 의학기술: medical technology
10. 신체특성: body character
11. 발달시키다: to develop
12. 부분: part
13. 적절하다: be adequate
14. 침: needle
15. 감초: licorice
16. 쑥: mugwort
17. 인삼: ginseng
18. 녹용: deer antler
19. 약재: medicinal ingredients
20. 길러내다: to train, raise
21. 부족하다: to lack
22. 보충하다: to complement

Conversation 2 문병 와 줘서 고마워.

소연이는 영진이가 입원해 있는 병원으로 문병을 갔다.

Conversation 2

소연: 영진아!
영진: 어, 왔어?
소연: 많이 다쳤다고 그러던데 괜찮아?
영진: 허리를 좀 다쳤는데 이젠 거의 다 나았어.
소연: 입원했다는 소식 듣고 너무 놀랐어.
어떻게 하다가 사고가 난 거야?
영진: 앞에 가는 트럭에서 박스가 떨어져서
피하려다가[G12.3] 사고가 났어.
소연: 많이 놀랐겠구나.[G12.4] 다른 데는 괜찮대?
영진: 응, 의사 선생님이 삼 일 후엔 퇴원할 수 있대.
안전 벨트 안 했으면 더 크게 다쳤을 거야.
소연: 다행이다.
영진: 바쁠 텐데 이렇게 와 줘서 고마워.
소연: 당연히 와야지. 치료 잘 받고 몸조리 잘 해.
그리고 뭐 필요한 거 있으면 언제든지[G12.5] 연락해.
영진: 그래, 고마워.

COMPREHENSION QUESTIONS

1. 소연이는 어디에 갔습니까?
2. 영진이는 무슨 일이 있었습니까?
3. 영진이에게는 무엇이 다행입니까?

NEW WORDS

NOUN

관계	relationship
느낌	feeling, sense
다이어트	diet
문병(하다)	visit (someone sick)
소문	rumor
안전 벨트	seat belt
위	stomach
이상	abnormality
입원(하다)	hospitalization
치료(하다)	treatment
퇴원(하다)	discharge (hospital)
팔	arm
허리	waist, back

SUFFIX

~(으)려다가	about to but then
~(이)든지	any . . .
~ 군요/구나	speaker's new discovery

VERB

낫다	to recover
놀라다	to be startled
떨어지다	to fall
생기다	to be formed
줄이다	to decrease
피하다	to avoid

ADJECTIVE

가능하다	be possible
규칙적(이다)	be regular
깊다	be deep
적당하다	be adequate
젊다	be young

ADVERB

거의	almost
되도록	as . . . as possible
지속적으로	consistently

NEW EXPRESSIONS

1. 다치다 'to hurt' is a transitive verb when it takes an object as in (a). It is also used as an intransitive verb as in (b).

(a) 나는 어제 다리를 다쳤다. I hurt my leg yesterday.
(b) 내가 좀 다쳤다. I hurt myself.

2. 다쳤다고 하던데 'they say that you were hurt/I hear that you were hurt' involves an indirect quotation pattern (G6.3). This phrase can be simplified as 다쳤다던데.

3. 입원했다는 소식 'the news that (you) got hospitalized': A sentence is followed by the suffix ~는 to modify a noun.

4. 몸조리 'recuperation, care of health'. 몸조리하다 'to take good care of one's health'. 몸조리 잘 해 is a fixed expression addressed to someone who is sick.

Grammar

G12.3 ~(으)려다가 'about to . . . but then . . .'

Examples

(1) 성희: 어떻게 된 거예요?
영진: 앞에서 오는 차를 피하**려다가** 사고가 났어요.

(2) 민지: 성희야, 방학 때 계절학기 들어?
성희: 응. 수업 세 개 들**으려다가** 너무 힘들 것 같아서 그냥 두 개로 줄였어.
I was going to take three classes, but it seemed too difficult, so I'll be taking just two.

(3) 민지: 소연아! 병원에는 웬일이야?
소연: 어, 민지야.
다이어트 하**려다가** 식사를 못해서 위가 안 좋아졌어.
민지: 그랬구나. 되도록 식사를 규칙적으로 해야지.

(4) 영진: 민지가 무슨 말 **할라 그러다가** 그냥 끊어 버리네요.
혹시 무슨 얘기인지 알아요?
성희: 민지랑 민호랑 사귄다는 소문이 있나 봐요.

Notes

1. Recall that ~다가 indicates that he/she shifts momentum from one action to another, and that ~(으)려고 indicates that he/she is about to do or try to do something. Combined, ~(으)려다가 is used to describe a situation where he/she is about to do or try to do something but runs into another situation.

2. ~(으)려다가 as in (1)~(3) is contracted from ~(으)려고 + 하다가. In colloquial speech, many people say ~(으)ㄹ라 그러다가 as in (4) instead of ~(으)려고 하다가.

Exercises

Complete the dialogues using ~(으)려다가 or ~(으)ㄹ라 그러다가.

(1) 성희: 어떻게 하다가 차사고가 났어요?
　　영진: 옆에서 오는 차를 피하려다가 그랬어요.

(2) A: 어제 왜 스티브 생일 파티에 안 왔어요?
　　B: ________________________________.

(3) A: 어떻게 하다가 팔을 다쳤어요?
　　B: ________________________________.

(4) A: 선생님께서 무슨 말씀 없으셨어요?
　　B: ________________________________.

(5) A: '토이스토리 4' 아직 안 보셨어요?
　　B: ________________________________.

G12.4 Expressing new discovery: ~군요/구나

Examples

(1) 민지: 수빈아, 그동안 학교에 왜 안 나왔어?
수빈: 기침이 심해서 3일 동안 집에 있었어.
민지: 많이 힘들어겠**구나**!

(2) [영진 is making a phone call to 성희, although he is not sure if 성희 is at home]
성희: 여보세요.
영진: 어, 성희야. 집에 있었**구나**! 나 영진이야.

(3) A: 내 동생이 다음 주에 결혼해요.
B: 어렸을 때 봤었는데 벌써 어른이 다 됐**군요**!

 Notes

1. ~군요/구나 is an exclamatory expression that is used when something new enters the speaker's consciousness. The statement expressed with ~군요/구나 is not a factual statement from the speaker's prior knowledge, but an immediate reaction to what has just been perceived.

2. ~군요 is used in the polite speech style, and ~구나 in the plain speech style as in (1) and (2).

3. The speaker can refer to the perception he/she received in the past with ~더군요. In this case, the speaker is referring to that moment in the past when the perception was made.

4. Recall that ~네(요) (Korean 1, Lesson 10, G10.4) can also be used in expressing what the speaker has just recognized. There is a subtle difference, however, between ~군요 and ~네요. What the speaker has just recognized in the case of ~군요 is a simple perception. What the speaker has just recognized in the case of ~네요, on the other hand, is more like surprise, usually contrary to what the speaker was expecting.

Exercises

Using ~군요, give an exclamatory statement that is appropriate for the given situation.

(1) [Seeing someone who recently got a haircut]

______________________________!

(2) 의사: 어떻게 오셨어요?

영진: 농구('basketball') 하다가 넘어졌는데요. 그 다음부터 걸을 수가 없어요.

의사: ______________________________!

(3) [Noticing the other person's hand is wrapped in a bandage]

______________________________!

(4) [Noticing that patients are lined up to see the doctor]

영진: ______________________________!

의사: 네, 오늘은 주말이라서 좀 많군요.

(5) [Noticing that your friend is searching for hotels online]

A: ______________________________!

B: 응, 좋은 호텔이 너무 많아서 아직 못 정했어.

Notes

G12.5 Indefinite pronouns ~(이)든지 'any . . .'

Examples

(1) A: 내일 몇 시쯤 놀러 갈까요?
B: 저는 하루 종일 집에 있을 거니까 **언제든지** 놀러 오세요.

(2) A: 스티브 씨는 한국 음식을 좋아하나 봐요.
B: 먹는 것은 **뭐든지** 잘 먹어요.

(3) A: 오늘 민속박물관에 가 볼래요? 한복을 입은 사람은 **누구든지** 공짜로 박물관에 들어갈 수 있대요.
B: 그래요? 그럼 한복을 입고 가야 되잖아요. 난 한복이 없는데.

(4) 우리는 아직 젊기 때문에 **무엇이든지** 할 수 있다.

(5) 서울에서 **어디든지** 가 보고 싶은 곳이 있으면 말씀하세요.

Notes

1. The particle ~(이)든지 is attached to a question/indefinite word such as 무엇 'what; something', 누구 'who; someone', or 언제 'when; some time', to mean 'any . . .', as in:

무엇이든지	anything	누구든지 anybody
언제든지	any time	어디든지 any place

2. ~(이)든지 is mostly interchangeable with 아무 . . . ~(이)나:

무엇이든지 = 아무거나	누구든지 = 아무나
언제든지 = 아무 때나	어디든지 = 아무 데나

3. Note that 이든지 occurs after a consonant and 든지 after a vowel.

Exercises

Fill in the blanks with an appropriate expression: 뭐든지, 누구든지, 언제든지, 어디든지.

(1) 민지: 아무것도 안 먹는데 배가 부른 느낌이에요.
병원: 증상이 계속 되면 언제든지 진찰 받으러 오세요.

(2) (식당에서)
A: 뭐 드실래요?
B: 저는 한국 음식은 ____________다 잘 먹습니다.

(3) A: 교수님, 내일 연구실에 몇 시쯤 갈까요?
B: 오전에는 ____________ 좋아요.

(4) A: 졸업 여행을 계획하고 있는데 어디가 적당할까요?
B: 저는 바닷가 근처라면 ____________ 괜찮은 것 같은데요.

(5) A: 스트레스와 건강은 깊은 관계가 있나요?
B: 물론이죠. ____________ 지속적으로 스트레스를 받으면 몸에 이상이 생겨요.

(6) A: 아르바이트 학생을 구하시지요?
B: 네.
A: 어떤 학생을 구하세요?
B: 한국말을 잘하는 학생이라면 ____________ 다 가능합니다.

Narration 건강한 생활

건강하게 오래 사는 것은 모든 사람들이 원하는 일이다. 건강은 건강할 때 지켜야 한다는 말이 있다. 건강이 나빠진 후에 치료하는 것보다 병에 걸리지 않게 조심하는 것이 더 중요하다. 건강하게 살기 위해서는 스트레스를 줄이고 즐겁게 살아야 한다. 많이 웃는 것도 건강에 좋다. 그래서 한국에는 "웃으면 복이 온다"는 말도 있다. 그리고 건강을 위해서[1] 규칙적인 생활을 해야 한다. 특히 적당한 운동과 휴식이 필요하다. 음식도 건강과 깊은 관계가 있다. 한국 사람들은 짜고 매운 음식을 좋아하기 때문에 위가 나쁜 사람들이 많은 편이다. 건강을 위해서는 가능하면 싱겁게 먹는 것이 좋다.

1. [Noun]을 위해서: 'for (the sake of)'

COMPREHENSION QUESTIONS

1. 건강하게 살려면 어떻게 해야 합니까?
2. 건강과 웃음은 어떤 관계가 있습니까?
3. 건강과 음식은 어떤 관계가 있습니까?

NEW EXPRESSIONS

1. 줄이다 'to reduce (something)' is a transitive verb and 줄다 'to be reduced' is an intransitive verb.

스트레스를 줄이려고 수영을 해요.	I swim in order to reduce stress.
매일 조깅을 하니까 스트레스가 줄었다.	Because I jog every day, my stress was reduced.

2. 짜다 'be salty', 맵다 'be spicy', 싱겁다 'be bland'

Notes

USAGE

1 *Describing illnesses and injuries*

Practice the following conversations.

(1) At a hospital

의사: 어디가 불편하세요?
민지: 배가 자꾸 아프고 소화가 안 돼요.
의사: 어제 뭐 드셨어요?
민지: 친구 생일 파티에 갔다가 하도 맛있는 게 많아서 이것저것 많이 먹었어요.
의사: 어디 봅시다. (진찰을 한다.) 음, 체하셨네요. 아무리 맛있는 음식이라도 과식은 몸에 안 좋아요.

(2) At a dentist (치과에서)

성희: 자꾸 이가 아파요.
의사: 어디 봅시다. 자, 아 하세요. (치료한다.) 양치하세요.
성희: 어느 이가 썩었어요?
의사: 이가 썩어서 아픈 게 아니라 잇몸이 약해서 아픈 거예요.
성희: 잇몸이 안 좋아요?
의사: 네, 한 일주일 정도 치료 받으셔야 되겠는데요.
성희: 일주일이나요? 어휴, 저는 치과 오는 게 제일 무서운데요.
의사: 그래도 지금 치료 안 받으면 더 나빠져요.

(3) At a drugstore (약국에서)

마크: 기침이 심하게 나고 머리도 아픈데 약 좀 주세요.
약사: 열도 있으세요?
마크: 열은 별로 없는 것 같은데요.
약사: 기침은 언제부터 하셨어요?
마크: 사흘 정도 됐어요.
약사: 요즘 코감기가 유행인데 이 약을 잡숴 보세요.
마크: 이 약 먹으면 많이 졸려요?
약사: 아뇨. 이 약은 안 졸리는 약이에요.

Useful expressions

기침을 하다	to cough
진통제를 먹다	to take painkillers
진찰을 받다	to consult a doctor
토하다 (구토하다)	to vomit
설사하다	to have diarrhea
주사 맞다	to get a shot
체하다	to have an upset stomach
수술하다	to have surgery
엑스레이를 찍다	to take an X-ray/be X-rayed
속이 불편하다	to have digestive problems
이가/ 잇몸이 아프다	to have a toothache/gingivitis
이가 썩었다	to have tooth decay
열이 나다	to have a fever
코가 막히다	to have nasal congestion
목이 아프다	to have a sore throat
콧물이 나오다	to have a runny nose

Exercise 1

Interview your partner with the following questions.

(1) 병원에 입원해 본 적 있어요?
(2) 언제 제일 많이 아팠어요?
(3) 최근에 아파 본 적이 있어요?
(4) 규칙적인 운동을 하세요? 무슨 운동을 자주 하세요?
(5) 치과에 얼마나 자주 가세요?
(6) 감기에 걸렸을 때 어떻게 하면 빨리 나을 수 있어요?

 Exercise 2

Practice the conversations (1), (2), and (3) above again, changing the situations as follows.

(1) You had a stomachache since last night after eating too much at a buffet restaurant. Describe your symptoms to a doctor.
(2) You have a toothache. Call your dentist and describe your symptoms and then make an appointment to see him/her.
(3) You are in Seoul to visit a friend. You have a fever, nasal congestion, and headache pain. You want to buy a medicine at a drugstore. Describe each of your symptoms to a Korean pharmacist and request a non-drowsy medicine.

2 *Describing a car accident*

In pairs, practice the following conversation.

성희: 많이 다쳤다면서요? 영진 씨 괜찮아요?
영진: 성희 씨 왔어요? 허리를 약간 다쳤어요. 이젠 좀 나았어요.
성희: 입원했다는 소식 듣고 너무 놀랐어요. 어떻게 된 일이에요?
영진: 앞차가 빗길에 미끄러지는 바람에 피하려다가 벽을 받았어요.
성희: 저런, 다른 데는 이상 없대요?
영진: 네, 의사 선생님이 2주 후엔 퇴원 할 수 있대요.
성희: 몸조리 잘 하세요.
영진: 바쁜데 와 줘서 고마워요.
성희: 뭘요, 당연히 와야죠.

 Exercise 1

Practice the conversation again, changing the situations as follows.

(1) 영진 drove fast in the rain and hit the car in front of him.
(2) 영진 drove over the speed limit and hit another car.
(3) 영진 turned right on red without stopping and hit a car.
(4) A cat ran in front of 영진's car. He turned sharply and missed the cat. But his car hit a tree.

Useful expressions

속도 제한	a speed limit	빨간 불	a red light
파란 불	a green light	노란 불	a yellow light
차를 박다	to hit another car	오른쪽으로 돌다 /우회전하다	to turn right
왼쪽으로 돌다 /좌회전하다	to turn left	멈추다/서다	to stop a car
향수	homesick	호기심	curiosity
근교	the suburbs	위치	a location
장사	business	무료	free of charge
오천여점	about 5,000 pieces	유물	relics
고상하다	to be elegant	잔잔한	calm
광장	a plaza	연날리기	kite flying
줄넘기	jumping rope	기구	tools
주제	a theme	조선시대	Joseon dynasty
후기	later days	풍습	customs
야간	night	개장	opening
휴장	closing		

Exercise 2

Converse with your partner on the following topics.

(1) 교통 사고를 당해 본 적이 있어요? 어떻게 하다가 사고가 났어요?
(2) 교통 사고로 다쳐 본 적이 있어요? 얼마나 심하게 다쳤어요?
(3) 실수로 다른 차를 박아 본 적이 있어요? (실수 mistake, 박다 to crash) 어떻게 사고를 해결했어요? (해결하다 to solve)
(4) 차사고가 나는 원인 3가지만 말해 보세요. (원인 cause)

Exercise 3

Role play

(1) You had a car accident recently. Your friend wants to know when and where the accident took place and how it happened.

(2) You witnessed a car accident at an intersection in Seoul. Explain to a police officer (경찰) that the driver who is responsible for the accident ran a red light and hit the other car.

Exercise 4

Role-play a conversation between a police officer and a driver based on the following situations:

(1) The driver was driving under the influence of alcohol.

(2) The driver wasn't wearing a seat belt.

(3) The driver didn't stop at a stop sign.

Notes

Lesson 12. Hospitals and Drugstores

CONVERSATION 1 *What Seems to Be the Problem?*

Minji goes to the hospital because she is sick.

Doctor: What seems to be the problem?

Minji: I have a mild fever and severe cough. It hurts so bad I haven't been able to eat anything.

Doctor: Do you have any other symptoms?

Minji: I've been having trouble with my digestion for the past three days.

Doctor: Let's take a look.

The doctor examines her.

Minji: Is it really bad?

Doctor: You caught a severe flu. Your throat is sore because you've been coughing so much.

Minji: I should have come a bit sooner.

Doctor: Well, I'm going to prescribe two days' worth of medicine for you, so please take it and get plenty of rest.

Minji: Okay, I will.

A bit later at the pharmacy nearby the hospital.

Pharmacist: Here is your medicine. Take one pill after meals three times per day. You need to take it on time.

Minji: Will it make me drowsy?

Pharmacist: No, you should be fine.

CONVERSATION 2 *Thank You for Visiting Me.*

Soyeon went to visit Youngjin at the hospital.

Soyeon: Youngjin!

Youngjin: Hey, look who made it.

Soyeon: I heard you got hurt pretty bad. Are you alright?

Youngjin: I hurt my waist a little, but it's almost better now.

Soyeon: I was so surprised when I heard the news that you were hospitalized. How did the accident happen?

Youngjin: I got into an accident trying to avoid a box that fell off of a truck that was in front of me.

Soyeon: You must have been shocked. Did they say everything else is fine?

Youngjin: Yes, my doctor said I can be discharged in three days. I would have been hurt much more if I hadn't had the seat belt on.

Soyeon: Oh, that's good.

Youngjin: You must be busy, so thank you for coming to see me like this.

Soyeon: Of course. Take good care of yourself and get well soon with your treatment. And just give me a call if you need anything.

Youngjin: Okay, thank you.

NARRATION *Western Medicine and Oriental Medicine*

Living a long and healthy life is something everyone wants. It is said that health is something that needs to be maintained when you are healthy. It is more important to be careful of catching an illness than to get treated after your health has already declined. In order to live healthily, you should reduce your stress and enjoy life. Laughing often is also good for your health. That's why in Korea there's the saying "laughter brings luck." Also for the sake of your health, you need to have a routine. A proper amount of exercise and rest are especially important. Food also has a close relationship with health. Because Koreans like salty and spicy food, there are many people with stomach issues. For your health, it is good to eat bland food.

CULTURE *Western Medicine and Oriental Medicine*

Before Western medicine was introduced to Korea in the 20th century, a traditional medical practice called "Oriental medicine" was the only method for treating people's illnesses and improving their health. Oriental medicine typically consists of herbal tonics and acupuncture; it was developed based on ancient Chinese medical technology to match the Korean body.

Acupuncture is when a needle is put into the proper area of the 356 areas on the body. And Oriental doctors prescribe medicine made up of medical ingredients like licorice, mugwort, ginseng, and deer antlers. There are even Oriental medicine universities that train Oriental doctors. Many Koreans supplement Western medicine's shortcomings with Oriental medicine.

13과 문화 차이

Lesson 13 Cultural Differences

Conversation 1 한국 문화는 알면 알수록 재미있어요.

스티브가 하숙집에서 아침을 먹고 나서 아주머니하고 얘기하고 있다.

Conversation 1

스티브: 아주머니, 밥 잘 먹었습니다.

아주머니: 스티브는 그동안 한국어 실력이 많이 는 것 같네.

스티브: 글쎄요, 저는 한국어가 생각만큼 안 늘어서 걱정인데요. 특히 한국 문화는 아직도 잘 모르겠어요. 한국에서 일 년이나 살았는데도[G13.1] 아직 실수를 많이 해요.

아주머니: 어떤 실수?

스티브: 처음 한국 친구 집에 놀러 갔을 때 저 혼자 신발을 신고 들어갔어요.

아주머니: 아, 그랬어? 스티브가 몰랐구나.

스티브: 아주머니 또 궁금한 게 하나 있는데요.

아주머니: 뭔데?

스티브: 한국에서는 병원 엘리베이터에 왜 4 대신 'F'라고 되어 있어요?

아주머니: 아, 그건 4(사)가 한자어로 '죽다(사:死)'라는 뜻의 한자하고 발음이 같아서 그래.

스티브: 아, 그렇군요. 한국 문화는 알면 알수록[G13.2] 참 재미있는 것 같아요.

COMPREHENSION QUESTIONS

1. 스티브는 한국 생활에서 어려운 부분이 무엇이라고 합니까?
2. 스티브는 친구 집에서 어떤 실수를 했습니까?
3. 스티브는 아주머니에게 무엇을 물어봤습니까?
4. 아주머니는 무슨 대답을 해 주셨습니까?

NEW WORDS

NOUN

논문	thesis
대신	instead of
동창	alumni
뜻	meaning
문명	civilization
발달(하다)	development
발음	pronunciation
방법	method
실력	skill, ability
실수(하다)	mistake
의미(하다)	signification
인간	human being
정	affection
차이	difference
한자	Chinese character
한자어	Sino-Korean word
회식	get-together (work)

VERB

나누다	to share
늘다	to increase
빠지다	to drop/leave out
살이 찌다	to gain weight
일어서다	to stand up
(시간이) 지나다	to pass, go by

ADJECTIVE

궁금하다	be curious

ADVERB

왜냐하면	because, since

PARTICLE

만큼	as . . . as

SUFFIX

~(으)면 (으)ㄹ수록	the more . . . the more
~(으)/는데도	despite the fact that

NEW EXPRESSIONS

1. 실력이 많이 늘다 'to improve one's proficiency', where 실력 means 'ability, proficiency' and 늘다 'to increase'.

2. 한국어가 생각만큼 안 늘어요. The particle 만큼 in 생각만큼 means 'not as much as I thought it would . . .'.

3. 4가 한자어로 '죽다'라는 뜻: The Korean vocabulary has a large percentage of words derived from Chinese (한자어). There are many homonyms; 사 ('number four' 四) and 사 ('death' 死) are pronounced the same but have different meanings and the Chinese characters are different.

Grammar

G13.1 ~는/(으)ㄴ데도 'despite the fact that'

Examples

(1) 한자 공부를 많이 했**는데도** 단어의 의미를 잘 모르겠다. — Despite the fact that I studied Chinese characters a lot, I still don't know the meaning of the words.

(2) A: 한국 시장에 와 보니까 어때요?
B: 정말 싸네요. 이렇게 많이 샀**는데도** 4만 원밖에 안 해요. — It's really cheap. Despite the fact that I bought this much, it was only 40,000 won.

(3) A: 늦은 시간**인데도** 회식에 안 빠졌네요. — Despite the late hour, you didn't miss the gathering.
B: 내일이 휴일이잖아요.

(4) A: 와, 월요일**인데도** 식당에 사람이 많네요!
B: 동창회 모임이 있어서 그래요.

Notes

Recall that ~는데/(으)ㄴ데 refers to a background circumstance against which a main event is described, often in contrast with it. 도 indicates that another item is added to the already existing list of items. Combined together, ~는/(으)ㄴ데도 is used to express that a main event unexpectedly takes place even under a background circumstance under which the main event normally does not take place. It can be translated as "despite the fact that . . .".

Exercises

Using ~는/(으)ㄴ데도, make up a dialogue according to the given context.

(1) [B is a big eater, but still in good shape. A sees B eating.]
A: 그렇게 많이 먹는데도 살이 안 찌는 방법이 뭐예요?
B: 매일 운동을 해요.

(2) [On a Sunday brunch]
소연: 성희야, 왜 벌써 일어서?
성희: 응, 도서관에 가는데.
소연: ________________________ 도서관에 가니?
성희: 응, 내일 시험이 있어서.

(3) [On a rainy day]
소연: 스티브 씨, 야구 구경 안 갈래요?
스티브: ________________ 야구를 해요?
소연: 네. 지붕이 있거든요. (지붕 roof)

(4) [Witnessing a small kid beating his big brother]
A: ______________________ 농구를 잘하네요.
B: 키는 작지만 빠르잖아요.

(5) [성희 knows that 소연 stayed up very late last night.]
성희: 소연아 잘 시간 지났는데 졸리지 않니?
소연: 응, ______________________ 안 졸리네.

G13.2 (~(으)면) . . . ~(으)ㄹ수록 'the more . . . , the more . . .'

Examples

(1) 민호: 마크 씨, 한국어 참 잘 하시네요.
마크: 아니에요. 한국어는 **하면 할수록** 어려운 것 같아요. — The more I learn Korean, the more difficult it seems.

(2) 민호: 소연 씨는 어느 배우를 좋아하세요?
소연: 저는 조니 뎁을 좋아해요. **보면 볼수록** 멋있어요. — The more I look at him, the better he looks.
민호: 그래요? 저는 숀펜이 좋아요. 왜냐하면, 나이가 **(들면) 들수록** 더 멋있어지는 것 같거든요. — I like Sean Penn because the more he ages, the more stylish he becomes.

(3) 민호: 마크 씨, 별일 없죠? 좀 피곤해 보여서요.
마크: 논문 쓰느라고 그래요. 요즘은 **(자면) 잘수록** 더 졸려요.

(4) 문명이 발달**하면 할수록** 인간 관계에서 정이 없어지는 것 같다.

Notes

1. In ~(으)면 . . . ~(으)ㄹ수록 'the more . . . , the more . . .', the ~(으)면 part can be omitted as in (2) and (3).

2. For 하다 verbs and adjectives such as 공부하다 and 행복하다, the noun part 공부 and 행복 can be omitted in the ~(으)ㄹ수록 part as in (4).

공부하면 할수록 행복하면 할수록

3. Fixed expressions:

될수록	(as much) as possible
갈수록 태산이다	run into deeper and deeper trouble/obstacle

Exercises

1. Using (~(으)면) . . . ~(으)ㄹ수록, make up an expression that fits the given entity.

(1) 농구할 때는 키가 크면 클수록 좋다.
(2) 돈은 ______________________________ 좋다.
(3) 수지는 ______________________________ 예쁘다.
(4) 도시는 ______________________________ 좋다.
(5) 외국어는 ______________________________ 좋다.

2. Fill in the blank with an entity that fits the description.

(1) 자동차는 크면 클수록 좋다.
(2) __________은/는 길면 길수록 좋다.
(3) __________은/는 짧으면 짧을수록 좋다.
(4) __________은/는 빠르면 빠를수록 좋다.
(5) __________은/는 보면 볼수록 좋다.
(6) __________은/는 부르면 부를수록 좋다.
(7) __________은/는 나누면 나눌수록 좋다.

Notes

Conversation 2 수업에 지각할 뻔 했어요.

소연과 스티브가 학교에서 오랜만에 만났다.

Conversation 2

소연: 스티브 씨, 요즘 좀 피곤해 보이네요.

스티브: 과제 때문에 계속 늦게 자서 그런가 봐요.
어제도 밤새 작업을 하다가 잠깐 잠들었는데
아침에 늦게 일어나는 바람에 수업에 지각할
뻔했어요.[G13.3]
소연 씨한테 하나 물어 볼 게 있는데요.

소연: 뭔데요?

스티브: 지난주에 아는 교수님 댁에 놀러 갔더니[G13.4]
식구가 일곱 명이나 되더라고요. 할아버지,
할머니, 교수님 부부, 그리고 직장에 다니는
아들, 대학교에 다니는 딸 둘, 이렇게 일곱 명이
다 한집에 살던데요.

소연: 그게 이상해 보였어요?
스티브: 약간이요. 미국에서는 자녀들이 대학교에 들어가면서부터 보통 따로 살거든요.
소연: 그렇죠, 그런데 한국에서는 결혼하기 전까지 보통 부모님과 같이 살아요. 결혼하고 나서도 부모님과 같이 살기도 해요.
스티브: 아, 그렇군요.

COMPREHENSION QUESTIONS

1. 스티브는 왜 요즘 늦게까지 잠을 못 잡니까?
2. 스티브는 아는 교수님 댁의 어떤 것이 이상하다고 생각합니까?
3. 소연이는 한국 문화에 대해 어떤 설명을 해 주었습니까?

NEW WORDS

NOUN

과제	assignment
관련	relation, connection
동아리	(social) club, group
목욕탕	public bathhouse
반말(하다)	informal/impolite talk
밤새	all night long
별일	anything particular
부부	married couple
불	light; fire
식구	family member
이웃	neighbor, neighborhood
자녀	children
점	point, aspect
지각(하다)	lateness
찻길	street, road

VERB

놓치다	to miss, lose
당황하다	to fluster
맞추다	to set, adjust
변하다	to change, alter
잠들다	to fall asleep

ADJECTIVE

이상하다	be strange, odd

ADVERB

다행히	fortunately
하마터면	almost
함께	together

SUFFIX

~(으)ㄹ 뻔하다	almost happened
~었/았더니	I did . . . and then

NEW EXPRESSIONS

~는 바람에 'because, as a result of' refers to forceful effects of one situation on another, and is used to give a reason or an explanation for the situation at hand. The effects expressed with this expression are incidental, indirect, and generally negative.

차사고가 나는 바람에 허리를 다쳤어요.

Grammar

G13.3 ~(으)ㄹ 뻔하다 'almost happened'

Examples

(1)	민호:	마크 씨, 좀 피곤해 보이네요.	Mark, you look a little tired.
	마크:	어제 늦게 자서 그런가 봐요.	I guess it's because I went to bed late yesterday.
		오늘도 아침 수업에 늦**을 뻔했어요**.	I was almost late for class this morning too.
		버스를 놓쳤거든요.	

(2) 마크: 오늘 큰일 **날 뻔 했어요**.
민호: 왜요?
마크: 학교 오늘 길에 사고가 **날 뻔 했어요**.
학교에 늦어서 급하게 오다가 빨간 불을 못 보고
그냥 지나갔어요.

(3) 대학 동아리 모임에서 등산을 갔다가 넘어져서 다**칠 뻔했어요.**

(4) 학교 화장실에 두고 나온 지갑을 어떤 학생이 사무실로 가지고 왔더라고요. 하마터면 지갑을 잃어버**릴 뻔했어요**.

Notes

1. ~(으)ㄹ 뻔하다 indicates that some event almost happened.
2. ~(으)ㄹ 뻔하다 is used always in the past tense, e.g., ~(으)ㄹ 뻔했어요.
3. The event in question did not take place; hence the prospective (non-realized) noun-modifying form ~(으)ㄹ is used.

Exercises

Using ~(으)ㄹ 뻔하다, complete the given utterances or sentences.

(1) 아침에 늦게 일어나서 지각할 뻔했어요.

(2) A: 오늘은 학교에 안 늦었어요?
B: 네, 다행히 시간 맞춰 버스를 탔어요.
그 버스 놓쳤으면 ________________.

(3) 계단 조심하세요. 저도 지난번에 ____________.

(4) 오늘 아침에 운전하고 가는데 이웃에 사는 아이가 갑자기 찻길로 뛰어들어서 잘못하면 아이가 ________________.

(5) A: 안 나가세요? 3시에 약속 있다고 그랬잖아요?
B: 아 참, ____________. 고마워요.

G13.4 ~었/았더니 'I did . . . and then . . .'

Examples

(1) 민지: 마크 씨, 한국에서 살면서 이상한 점 혹시 없어요?
마크: 있죠. 지난주에 아는 교수님 댁에 **갔더니** 식구가 7명이나 되더라고요. 그래서 어떻게 이렇게 많은 식구가 함께 사느냐고 **했더니** 좀 변하기는 했지만 한국에서는 식구가 같이 모여 사는 것이 전통이라고 하시더라고요.

(2) 내가 제니한테 같이 목욕탕에 가자고 **했더니** 많이 당황하더라고요.

(3) 어제 출근 시간에 버스를 **탔더니** 사람이 너무 많아서 서 있을 자리도 없었다. I got on the bus during the rush hour yesterday, and (I recall that) there were so many people, there was no place to stand.

(4) 오래간만에 테니스를 **쳤더니** 굉장히 피곤해요. As I played tennis for the first time in a long time, I'm very tired.

Notes

1. ~었/았더니 is used to describe a situation when the speaker came to experience in the past as a result of or in reaction to another situation. The conditioning situation is mostly his/her own (not another person's).

2. As in (1) and (2) a sentence with ~었/았더니 usually contains the ~더라구(요) ending.

Exercises

1. Using ~었/았더니, complete the given sentences.

(1) 오래간만에 테니스를 쳤더니 피곤해요.
(2) 배고프다고 ________________ 빵을 나누어 주었어요.
(3) 아침에 일어나서 ______________ 눈이 하얗게 쌓여 있더라고요.
(4) 옆집 사람한테 반말을 ____________ 화를 내더라고요.
(5) 지난주에 월급을 받았는데 _____________ 벌써 돈이 다 없어졌어요.

2. Complete the following sentences.

(1) 오래간만에 테니스를 쳤더니 피곤해요.
(2) 어제 커피를 많이 마셨더니 __________________________.
(3) 어제 잠을 못 잤더니 ________________________________.
(4) 수지가 학교에 안 와서 전화를 했더니 _________________.
(5) 약속 시간에 30분쯤 늦게 갔더니 ____________________.

Notes

Narration 스티브의 한국 생활

스티브가 한국 생활을 한 지 벌써 일년이 다 되었다. 처음에 한국에 왔을 때는 문화가 많이 달라서 불편한 점도 많았지만 지금은 적응이 되었다.

한국 사람들은 인간 관계를 아주 중요하게 생각하는 것 같다. 좋은 인간 관계를 위해서 모임도 자주 갖고 음식을 함께 먹는 것을 중요하게 생각한다. 스티브도 친구들 모임이나 동아리 모임에 많이 가 봤다. 한국 사람들은 동창 모임도 자주 갖고, 직장에서도 회식을 자주 한다고 한다. 그런데 이런 자리에는 술과 음식이 빠지지 않는다. 그래서 음식하고 관련된 재미있는 한국 문화도 많다. 스티브는 한국 사람들이 찌개나 반찬을 가운데 놓고 같이 먹는 것을 보고 처음에는 많이 당황했었다.

그렇지만 지금은 서로 나누어 먹어야 정이 더 생긴다는 한국 문화를 이해하게 되었다. 재미있는 것은, 가족을 의미하는 '식구(食口)'라는 단어도 밥을 함께 먹는 사람이라는 뜻이다. 인사를 할 때도 '식사하셨어요?' 혹은 '밥 먹었어요?'라고 묻기도 한다. 한국인에게 음식은 사람들 사이에 정을 나누는 좋은 방법인 것 같다.

COMPREHENSION QUESTIONS

1. 스티브는 왜 처음에 한국 생활이 불편했었습니까?
2. 한국에서는 인간 관계에서 어떤 것이 중요합니까?
3. 스티브는 한국 문화의 어떤 것 때문에 당황했었습니까?
4. 스티브가 한국의 가족과 음식에 대해 이해하게 된 것은 무엇입니까?

NEW EXPRESSIONS

Both 동아리 and 동우회/동호회 refer to meetings of people with the same objective, goal, hobby, interest, etc. The first one is usually used for college groups, whereas the second is used for people in general.

CULTURE

미신 Superstition

음력 새해 초[1]에 사람들은 새해 운세[2]를 본다. 이 기간[3] 동안 거리 곳곳[4]이나 시장에는 토정비결[5] 책을 놓고 손님들을 기다리는 점술인[6]들을 보게 된다. 가끔은 미신 취급[7]을 받기도 하지만 토정비결은 여전히 사람들에게 사랑을 받고 있다. 사람들은 점술인을 찾아가서 시험, 사업[8], 결혼 등 인생의 중대사[9]에 대해서 상담[10]을 한다.

풍수는 도시나 집을 지을[11] 때, 혹은 묘지[12]를 정할 때 기운[13]이 좋은 곳을 선정[14]하기 위한 토정비결의 방법입니다. 토정비결에서는 이상적인 위치에 들어선[15] 집에서는 행복과 번영이 가득[16]할 것이라고 믿는다.

1. 초: beginning
2. 운세: fortune
3. 기간: period
4. 곳곳: everywhere
5. 토정비결: *Tojung* Secret (book)
6. 점술인: fortune-teller
7. 취급: treatment
8. 사업: business
9. 중대사: serious matter
10. 상담: counseling
11. 짓다: to build
12. 묘지: cemetery
13. 기운: energy
14. 선정하다: to select
15. 들어서다: be built
16. 가득하다: be full of

USAGE

1 *Talking about cultural differences*

Practice the following conversations in pairs.

(1) Dinner invitation

마크: 그저께 친구 집에 저녁 초대받아 갔다가 깜짝 놀랐어요.
민호: 왜요? 무슨 일이 있었어요?
마크: 주인이 상다리가 부러지게 차렸는데도, '차린 건 없지만 많이 드세요' 라고 하더라고요.
민호: 네, 한국에서는 아무리 차린 게 많아도 보통 그렇게 말해요.
마크: 한국 문화는 알면 알수록 재미있는 것 같아요.

(2) Family system

마크: 어제 아는 교수님댁에 놀러 갔더니 식구가 7명이나 되더라고요. 대학교에 다니는 아들, 딸이 다 부모님하고 한집에 살던데요.
소연: 그게 이상해 보였어요?
마크: 약간요. 미국에서는 대학교 들어가면서부터 보통 따로 살거든요.
소연: 한국에서는 보통 한집에서 식구들이 다 같이 살아요.
마크: 같이 살면 불편하지 않아요?
소연: 힘든 점도 있지만 좋은 점도 있어요.

Exercise 1

Do you live with your parents? Discuss the advantages and disadvantages of living with parents.

Exercise 2

Have you noticed any differences between American and Korean cultures? Converse with your partner on the following topics and report the results to the class.

(1) Compliments and responding
(2) Giving and receiving presents/favors
(3) Dating and marriage
(4) Family system
(5) The use of kinship terms
(6) The use of body language/gestures

Exercise 3

Ask your partner when to use the following idiomatic expressions:

(1) 차린 건 없지만 많이 드세요.
(2) 상다리가 부러지게 차렸어요.
(3) 국수 언제 먹게 돼요?
(4) 이게 웬 떡이에요?
(5) 바가지 썼어요.
(6) 한잔합시다
(7) 바람 맞았어요.
(8) 발이 넓어요.
(9) 첫눈에 반했어요.

Exercise 4

Make an oral skit using at least one of the above expressions.

2 *Talking about Korean superstitions*

Here are some examples of Korean superstitions.

1. 돼지꿈 (to see a pig in a dream)—You will be rich.
2. 까치 (a magpie)—If you see a magpie in the morning, you will have a good visitor/guest.
3. 미역국 (seaweed soup)—If you eat seaweed soup on the day of a test, you will fail the test.
4. The number four (사)—a very unlucky number
5. 빨간 색 (red color)—You must not write people's names in red (unless for deceased people).

Exercise 1

Practice as in the example.

A: 한국 친구한테서 들었는데 [돼지꿈을 꾸면 부자가 된대요].
B: 그래요? 저는 처음 듣는 얘긴데요.

Now replace the bracketed part with the following superstitions and practice the dialogue again.

> 사다리 밑을 지나가면 재수가 없대요. (They say that if you walk under a ladder, you will have bad luck.)

New expressions

돼지	a pig	재수가 없다	to be unlucky
꿈	dream	시험에 떨어지다	to fail a test
꾸다	to dream		
사다리	a ladder		

(1) 아침에 까치가 울면 반가운 손님이 와요.
(2) 시험 보는 날 아침에 미역국을 먹으면 시험에 떨어져요.
(3) 숫자 4(사)는 재수가 없어요.
(4) 빨간 색으로 이름을 쓰면 안 돼요.

Exercise 2

Discuss more superstitions in your cultures.

2 *Narrating a series of events*

When you want to tell people a series of events or a story, it may be useful to utilize various narrative techniques, such as a variety of past tense forms, reportive styles, and sentence-ending forms. Here is an example of an extended narrative.

영진: 지난 겨울에 10년 만에 한국에 놀러 갔었어요.
샌디: 그랬어요? 재미있었겠네요.
영진: 네. 프랭크하고 같이 갔었어요. 그런데 서울이 너무 많이 변했더라고요. 공항에서 택시를 타고 시내로 가는데 길이 복잡하고 사람들이 하도 많아서 정신이 하나도 없었어요. 공항에서 내려서 할머니 댁으로 가다가 10년 전에 살던 동네를 지나가게 됐어요.

그런데 다른 건물들이 너무 많이 생겨서 제가 옛날에 살던 집은 찾기가 힘들더라고요. 10년 전에는 1층짜리 건물들이 많았었는데 지금은 모두 아파트가 되었어요.

The above dialogue can be rewritten in a written narrative style.

Exercise 1

Read the above narration and describe at least three changes that 영진 observed in Seoul.

Exercise 2

Reconstruct the following dialogue in a written narrative style.

유진: 마크 씨, 하숙집으로 이사했다면서요?
마크: 네. 아파트 주인이 방값을 올려서 하숙집으로 이사했어요.
아파트에 살 때보다 더 좋은 것 같아요. 하숙집 아주머니도 친절하시고
음식도 맛있어요. 그 전 집에서는 장보러 가기가 귀찮았는데
하숙집에서는 밥을 해 먹지 않으니까 참 편해요. 학교하고 가까워서
걸어갈 수도 있고 또 하숙집 친구들도 참 좋아요. 졸업할 때까지
이 하숙집에 지내려고 해요.

Exercise 3

Talk with your partner about a recent weekend, and then report to the class what your partner did in that weekend.

Exercise 4

Complete and reconstruct the following dialogues using the narrative style as shown in the example.

마크: 민호 씨, 이게 얼마 만이에요?
민호: 오래간만이에요. 그동안 어떻게 지내셨어요?

마크는 어제 오래간만에 우연히 민호를 만났다. 민호는 마크한테
조금 피곤해 보인다고 말했다. 마크는 요즘 논문 쓰느라고 계속
늦게 자서 그렇다고 했다. 민호는 마크의 한국어 실력이 많이
늘었다고 칭찬했다. 마크는 요즘 한국 사람을 만나면 꼭 한국말로만
이야기하려고 한다. 그저께는 미국 사람한테도 한국말로 이야기할
뻔했다.

(1) 성희: 이번 주말에 새로 나온 영화 보러 안 갈래요?
동수: 난 친구들하고 등산 가기로 벌써 약속을 했는데 . . .

(2) 마크: 다음 주 토요일이 성희 씨 결혼식이지요?
민지: 네, 결혼식장에 같이 갈래요?

Lesson 13. Cultural Differences

CONVERSATION 1 *Korean Culture Gets More Interesting the More I Learn.*

Steve is having a conversation with his landlord after breakfast at his rental house.

Steve: Thank you for breakfast.

Landlord: It seems your Korean has improved a lot, Steve.

Steve: I'm not so sure, I'm worried because my Korean isn't improving as fast as I thought it would. I especially don't know much about Korean culture. I'm still making so many mistakes despite having lived in Korea for a whole year.

Landlord: What kinds of mistakes?

Steve: The first time I visited a Korean friend's house I was the only one who entered while still wearing shoes.

Landlord: Oh, you did? You must not have known.

Steve: By the way, there's something else I'm curious about.

Landlord: What is it?

Steve: Why does it say 'F' instead of '4' in the hospital elevators in Korea?

Landlord: Oh, that is because the number four has the same pronunciation as the Sino-Korean word 'die'.

Steve: Oh, I see. I feel like Korean culture gets more and more interesting the more I know about it.

CONVERSATION 2 *I Was Almost Late for Class.*

Soyeon and Steve see each other for the first time in a while at school.

Soyeon: Steve, you look kind of tired lately.

Steve: It's probably because I've been going to sleep late due to school work. Even yesterday I fell asleep while I was up late working on an assignment, and was almost late to class because I woke up late this morning.

Steve: I have something to ask you, Soyeon.

Soyeon: What is it?

Steve: I went to a professor's house last week, and there were 7 relatives living together. Grandfather, grandmother, the professor and his wife, their working son, and their two daughters who are in college. All seven of them were living together in the same house.

Soyeon: Did that seem weird to you?

Steve: A little bit. In America, kids usually live separately once they go to college.

Soyeon: Right, but in Korea children normally live with their parents until they get married. Sometimes they keep living with their parents even after they get married.

Steve: Oh, I see.

NARRATION *Steve's Life in Korea*

It has been one year since Steve started living in Korea. When he first came to Korea, there were many things that he found uncomfortable due to cultural differences, but now he has adapted to these differences. Korean people seem to consider interpersonal relationships very important. They find eating together and having gatherings often important to keeping good relationships. Steve has also been to many gatherings with friends and with school clubs. It is said that Koreans also have many school reunions, and go out on many company dinners. In these kinds of events, food and alcohol are never left out. Because of this, there are a lot of interesting Korean cultural points related to food. Steve was very taken aback the first time he saw Korean people eating from the same dishes of soup and side dishes that were placed in the middle of them all. However now he understands the cultural point that you need to share food with each other in order to foster a deeper sense of brotherhood. An interesting point is that the Sino-Korean word for "family" means "people who eat together." And when people greet one another, they sometimes ask formally or informally "have you eaten?" To Koreans food seems like a good method for sharing a sense of brotherhood between people.

CULTURE *Superstitions*

At the beginning of the Lunar New Year, people predict their fortunes for the new year. During this period, people will start seeing fortune-tellers everywhere on the streets and in markets, waiting for clients with their *Tojung* Secret books in front of them. Occasionally, the *Tojung* Secret book is treated as a superstition, but it is still receiving love from people as much as ever. People will seek out fortune-tellers and get counseled on serious life matters, such as tests, business, and marriage.

Feng shui is a method of *Tojung* Secret that's used to select a place with good energy when building a city, house, or deciding on a cemetery. It's believed that houses in the ideal location within *Tojung* Secret will be full of happiness and prosperity.

Notes

14과 전공과 직업

Lesson 14 Majors and Jobs

Conversation 1 실수할까 봐 걱정이에요.

Conversation 1

민호: 소연 씨, 어디 가세요?

소연: 오늘 방송국 기자 면접이 있어서 방송국에 가는 길이에요.

민호: 그래요? 필기 시험에 붙었군요! 축하해요!

소연: 고마워요.

민호: 요즘 방송국에 취직하기가 하늘의 별 따기라면서요?[G14.1]

소연: 네. 공고가 나오자마자[G14.2] 몇 명 안 뽑는데 500명도 넘게 지원했대요.

민호: 그래요? 정말 경쟁이 심하네요.

소연: 근데 오늘 면접 시험에서 실수할까 봐[G14.3] 걱정이에요.

민호: 그래도 소연 씨는 필기 시험도 붙었고 적성도 방송 기자하고 잘 맞으니까 꼭 되실 거예요.

소연: 그랬으면 좋겠어요.

COMPREHENSION QUESTIONS

1. 소연이는 어디에 가는 길입니까?
2. 왜 방송국 취직이 하늘의 별따기라고 합니까?
3. 소연이는 무슨 걱정을 합니까?
4. 소연이는 어떤 일을, 왜 하고 싶어합니까?

NEW WORDS

NOUN		VERB	
경쟁(하다)	competition	넘다	to exceed
고민(하다)	worry	따다	to pick, pluck
공고	official announcement	떨어지다	to fail (the test)
과정	process	붙다	to pass (the test)
기자	reporter	뽑다	to single out
면접	interview	지원하다	to apply
별	star	**ADJECTIVE**	
사회	society	미끄럽다	be slippery
인생	(human) life	현명하다	be wise
재수(하다)	retake the exam	**ADVERB**	
적성	aptitude	마치	like, as if
직업	occupation, profession	**SUFFIX**	
필기 (시험)	written (exam)	~(으)ㄹ까 봐	'for fear that . . .'
학원	cram school	~다면서/라면서	confirming info
후회(하다)	regret	V.S.~자마자	'as soon as . . .'

NEW EXPRESSIONS

1. 하늘의 별 따기 'picking stars from the sky' means an impossible task.

2. 시험에 붙다 is a colloquial expression to mean 'to pass a test', and 시험에 떨어지다 'to fail a test'.

3. 꼭 되실 거예요. Here, 되다 means 'to turn out, get to be'.

   모든 일이 잘되었어요.
   잘될 거니까 걱정 마세요.

Grammar

G14.1 Confirming information: ~다면서?/라면서?

Examples

(1)	동수:	마크, 나야, 아까 나 없을 때 전화했**다면서**? 무슨 일이야?	Mark, it's me. I heard that you called a little while ago when I wasn't here. What's going on?
	마크:	응, 다른 게 아니고, 학원 숙제 때문에 전화했어.	Yeah, it's just that . . . I called because of homework from our cram school.
(2)	A:	방학 동안에 한국에 간**다면서요**?	I heard you're going to Korea during vacation.
	B:	네, 한국어를 배우러 가기로 했어요.	
(3)	A:	한국은 대학 입시 경쟁이 심하**다면서요**?	I heard the college entrance examination in Korea is very competitive.
	B:	네, 사실 내 친구도 이번에 재수해요.	Yes, in fact, a friend of mine will spend another year preparing for the exam.
(4)	A:	내일이 동수 씨 생일**이라면서요**?	
	B:	네, 저도 몰랐어요.	

Notes

~다면서(요)?/라면서(요)? is used to confirm information that the speaker has heard. It can be best translated into English as 'I heard . . . , is it true?'

~다면서: after a past suffix or adjective stem
~는/ㄴ다면서: after a verb stem
~(이)라면서: with the copula 이~ (e.g., 의사라면서?, 선생님이라면서?)

Exercises

1. Reconstruct the sentences using ~다면서(요).

(1) 어제 친구하고 등산 갔다 왔어요.
→ 어제 친구하고 등산 갔다 왔다면서요?

(2) 서울 교통이 아주 복잡해요.
______________________________.

(3) 요즘 공사 때문에 길이 많이 막혀요.
______________________________.

(4) 요즘은 취직이 마치 하늘의 별 따는 것처럼 어려워요.
______________________________.

(5) 한국 사회는 경쟁이 심해요.
______________________________.

(6) 지금 이 시간에는 지하철이 택시보다 더 빨라요.
______________________________.

Notes

Exercises

2. Based on the dialogue given in the [ ], complete the conversation in a way to confirm the information that was heard.

(1) [동수: 민지가 서울 간대.
스티브: 그래?]
스티브: 서울 간다면서요?
민지: 네, 방학 때 갔다오려고요.

(2) [유진: 내일 동수하고 등산 가기로 했어요.
스티브: 재미있겠네요.]
스티브: ______________________?
동수: 네. 유진이한테서 들으셨군요.

(3) [동수: 어제 뭐 했어?
스티브: 유진이하고 영화 봤어.]
동수: ______________________? 재미있었어?
유진: 응. 괜찮았어.

(4) [스티브: 유진이는 졸업하면 곧바로 취직한대?
동수: 그냥 대학원 지원하기로 했대.]
스티브: 졸업하고 나서 ______________________?
무슨 공부할 거야?
유진: 글쎄, 아직 고민 중이야.

(5) [유진: 저, 동수 있어요?
동수 누나: 지금 없는데. 수영하러 가서 아직 안 왔는데.]
유진: 너 어제 ______________________?
동수: 응, 날씨가 더워서 오래간만에 했어.

G14.2 V.S.~자마자 'as soon as . . .'

Examples

(1)	우리 언니는 대학을 졸업하**자마자** 결혼했다.	My sister got married immediately after graduating from college.
(2)	소연: 민호 씨는 아침에 일어나면 제일 먼저 뭘 하세요? 민호: 저는 일어나**자마자** 물을 한 컵 마셔요.	
(3)	어제 너무 피곤해서 집에 오**자마자** 바로 잤다.	Yesterday, because I was so tired, I went right to bed as soon as I came home.

Notes

1. ~자마자 is equivalent to 'as soon as', 'no sooner than', or 'immediately after' in English.

2. ~자마자 is only attached to a verb.

3. It should be noted that 'as soon as' in English could mean something other than what ~자마자 in Korean can express. For example, the English sentence 'I will send my assignment as (soon as) I finish it' can be properly translated into Korean as 숙제 끝나는 대로 보내 드릴게요, rather than 숙제 끝나자마자 보내 드릴게요.

Notes

G14.3 ~(으)ㄹ까 봐 'for fear that . . .'

Examples

(1) A: 방송국 기자 시험 봤다면서요?
B: 네, 몇 주 전에 봤는데 떨어**질까 봐** 걱정이에요. — Yes, I took it a few weeks ago, but I'm worried for fear of failing.

(2) A: 왜 조금밖에 안 드세요?
B: 살**찔까 봐** 요즘 다이어트 중이에요. — For fear of gaining weight, I'm on a diet these days.

(3) 요즘 소화가 안 돼요. 밥만 먹으면 배가 아파요.
또 배가 아**플까 봐** 밥을 먹기가 싫어요.

(4) A: 졸업하고 나서 대학원 간다면서?
B: 응. 그런데, 나중에 후회**할까 봐** 걱정이야.
A: 인생 전체에서 대학원 과정은 2년밖에 안 되는데 뭐.
B: 아, 그래. 참 현명한 생각이구나.

Notes

This pattern is used when a person is worried, concerned, or afraid that something might happen. It can be translated as 'Worrying that . . .' or 'For fear of/that . . .'

Exercises

Make a dialogue using ~(으)ㄹ까 봐 as in the example.

(1) [Situation: 친구한테 전화하기로 했는데 밤 11시가 넘어서 못 했어요.]

A: 왜 어제 전화 안 했어요?

B: 자고 있을까 봐 안 했어요.

(2) [내일 아침 시험이 있어요. 그래서 일찍 일어나려고 일찍 자요.]

A: 왜 벌써 자려고 해요?

B: ______________________________.

(3) [눈이 와서 길이 미끄러워요. 넘어지지 않으려고 천천히 걸어요.]

A: 왜 그렇게 천천히 걸어요?

B: ______________________________.

(4) [차사고를 냈는데 부모님께 말씀 드리면 걱정하실 거예요.]

A: 왜 부모님께 말씀 드리지 않았어요?

B: ______________________________.

(5) [취직 시험을 봤는데 떨어질 것 같아요.]

A: 기분이 안 좋아 보여요. 무슨 일이 있어요?

B: ______________________________.

Conversation 2 경제와 관련된 일을 했으면 합니다.

소연이 면접장에 들어가서 자리에 앉는다.

Conversation 2

면접관 1: 간단하게 자기 소개 좀 해 보세요.

소연: 저는 한국 대학교 경제학과 4학년에 재학 중인 최소연입니다. 현재 저희 학교 신문 기자로 일하고 있습니다.

면접관 2: 좋습니다. 최소연 씨는 왜 우리 방송국에 지원했습니까?

소연: 이 방송국의 뉴스와 시사 프로그램이 아주 인상적이었습니다.

면접관 1: 기자가 된다면 어떤 분야에서 일하고 싶은지 생각해[G14.4] 보셨습니까?

소연: 제 전공이 경제학이라서 경제와 관련된 일을 했으면 합니다.[G14.5]

면접관 2: 기자가 본인 적성에 맞는다고 생각합니까?
소연: 제가 부전공으로 문학을 해서 글 쓰는 것을 있을 것 같습니다.
면접관 2: 네, 알겠습니다.

COMPREHENSION QUESTIONS

1. 소연이는 본인을 어떻게 소개했습니까?
2. 소연이는 왜 방송국에 지원을 하게 됐습니까?
3. 소연이는 어떤 분야에서 일하고 싶어합니까?
4. 소연이는 왜 이 일이 본인에게 잘 맞는다고 생각합니까?

NEW WORDS

NOUN

고3	high school senior
글	writing, composition
마음씨	heart, mind
면접관	interviewer
면접장	interview site
문학	literature
본인	self
부전공	minor
분야	area
삼촌	uncle
선택(하다)	choice, selection
시사	current affairs
입학(하다)	admission, entrance
자기 소개	self-introduction
자리	seat
작가	writer
재학 중	be in school
추천(하다)	recommend

VERB

관련되다	be related
기억나다/하다	to remember
무시하다	to ignore
(적성을) 살리다	to nurture (one's aptitude)
생각나다	be reminded
잘못하다	to do wrong

ADJECTIVE

마르다	be skinny

ADVERB

웬만하면	if possible

PARTICLE

같이	like, as

SUFFIX

~(으)ㄴ/는/(으)ㄹ지	wondering about
~었/았으면 하다	wish . . . ~ed

NEW EXPRESSIONS

~는 바람에 'because, as a result of' refers to forceful effects of one situation 1. 추천으로 'on the recommendation of . . .'

교수님 추천으로 도서관에 취직했습니다.

2. 적성에 맞다 'to have aptitude for, to have some talent in'

Grammar

G14.4 ~(으)ㄴ/는/(으)ㄹ지 (생각하다) 'wondering about'

Examples

(1) 삼촌: 성미야, 너도 이제 고3인데 대학 가서 뭘 공부**할지** **생각해** 봤니? — Now that you're a senior, have you thought about what you'll study in college?
성미: 글쎄요, 아직 뭘 해야 할지 잘 모르겠어요. — Well, I'm still not sure what I should do.

(2) 성미: 삼촌, 제가 뭐 잘못했어요?
삼촌: 모르겠어? 네가 뭘 잘못했**는지** 잘 **생각해** 봐.

(3) 소연: 민호 씨, 지수라고 키 크고 마른 여학생 알지요?
민호: 지수요? 알아요. 근데 키가 **큰지 작은지**는 잘 모르겠는데요.

(4) 성미: 소연아, 오늘 학교 도서관 몇 시에 여는지 아니?
소연: 글쎄, 방학이라서 **열지** 모르겠네.

Notes

1. ~(으)ㄴ/는/(으)ㄹ지 marks an indirect question that the speaker is wondering about or is not certain of.

2. It is usually followed by a verb or adjective of the following sort.

알다/모르다	to know/not know
기억하다/기억나다	to remember
생각해 보다	to think about
궁금하다	to be curious about

3. In the present tense, ~(으)ㄴ지 is used for adjectives and ~는지 for verbs. In the past tense, ~었/았는지 is used for both verbs and adjectives. ~(으)ㄹ지 is used for non-realized or prospective situations.

Exercises

Complete the given dialogues with ~(으)ㄴ/는/(으)ㄹ지.

(1) 소연: 민호 씨, 지수라고 왜 키 크고 마른 여학생 알지요?
민호: 지수요? 알아요. 근데 키가 큰지 작은지는 잘 모르겠는데요.

(2) 민호: 민지 씨, 이거 내일까지 해 올 수 있어요?
민지: 글쎄요, 하루 동안 ____________ 모르겠어요. 삼일은 있어야 할 것 같은데.

(3) 마크: 스티브 씨, 내가 끓인 커피 맛이 __________ 한번 드셔 보실래요?
스티브: 아, 괜찮은데요. 마크 씨가 커피를 이렇게 잘 끓이는 줄은 몰랐는데요.

(4) 마크: 스티브 씨, 새로 오신 한국어 선생님 예쁘세요?
민지: 글쎄요, 마음씨는 좋으신 것 같던데 ______________ 잘 모르겠는데요.

(5) 민지: 유진 씨, 언제 마지막으로 한국에 갔었어요?
유진: 글쎄요, _____________ 생각이 안 나는데요.

G14.5 ~었/았으면 하다 'wish . . . ~ed'

Examples

(1) 삼촌: 성미야, 너도 이제 고3인데 대학에 입학하면 뭘 공부할지 생각해 봤니?
성미: 글쎄요, 부모님은 경제학을 전공**했으면 하**시는데, 저는 문학을 전공하고 싶어요. 작가같이 혼자 일할 수 있는 직업이 좋아요.
Well, my parents want me to major in economics, but I want to major in literature.

(2) 남자: 결혼 후에도 일을 계속할 생각입니까?
소연: 네. 가능하면 결혼 후에도 일을 계속**했으면 합니다**.
남자: 어떤 일을 하고 싶습니까?
소연: 가능하면 제 전공을 살릴 수 있는 일을 **했으면 합니다**.

(3) 성희: 동수 씨, 오늘은 좀 일찍 들어 **왔으면 하**는데.
동수: 왜? 오늘 좀 바쁜데.
성희: 오늘 친구들 오기로 했잖아?

(4) 나는 대학생들이 전공을 선택할 때 자기 적성을 무시하지 않**았으면 한다**.

Notes

1. ~었/았으면 하다 is an expression of wish, functionally equivalent in English to 'wish . . . ~ed'

2. The content of the wish is expressed with a conditional clause in the past tense, that is, ~었/았으면. Note that in English too, the content of the wish is expressed in the past tense.

3. More informally, ~었/았으면 좋겠다 may be used, which literally means 'It would be good if . . .' It emphasizes one's personal feelings and there is less concern for the other party. ~었/았으면 하다 is more polite than ~(으)면 좋겠다 and can be used as an indirect request. For example,

> 선생님, 시험을 내일 봤으면 하는데요. 괜찮을까요?
> 기숙사보다는 아파트를 찾았으면 하는데요. 도와주세요.

Exercises

Complete the given utterance or sentence with an expression of a wish.

(1) 삼촌: 성미야, 대학 가서 뭘 공부할지 생각해 봤니?
성미: 글쎄요, 저는 문학을 전공했으면 해요.

(2) 유진: 소연 씨는 결혼한 후에도 계속 일할 생각이에요?
소연: 네, ________________________.

(3) 민호: 소연 씨는 졸업하고 어떤 일을 하고 싶어요?
소연: ________________________.

(4) 스티브: 마크 씨는 한국어 공부 끝나면 뭐 할 계획이에요?
마크: ________________________.

(5) 동수: 우리 이번 주말에 뭐 할까?
성희: 나는 ________________________.
오랫동안 부모님을 못 뵈었거든.

Narration 한국의 대학

한국에서 대학 입학은 아주 중요하다. 좋은 직장을 갖기 위해서는 대학을 나와야 된다고 생각한다. 그래서 고등학생들은 대학 입시를 준비하기 위해서 공부를 정말 열심히 한다. 그러다 보니 고등학교 생활은 대학을 들어가기 위한 준비 과정이 되어 버린다. 한국의 고등학생들은 학교 공부 외에도 학원에 가서 공부를 한다. 심지어는 대학에 떨어지고 나서 다음 해에 대학에 들어가기 위해서 재수를 하는 학생들도 있다.

대학에 들어갈 때 전공 선택이 아주 중요하다. 왜냐하면 전공에 따라 앞으로 인생이 크게 달라질 수 있기 때문이다. 그러나 적성을 무시하고, 조건만을 생각해서 전공을 선택하는 경우, 나중에 후회하게 될 수도 있다. 적성에 맞지 않는 일을 하는 것은 마치 발에 맞지 않는 신발을 신은 것같이 불편한 일이기 때문이다. 이런 점을 생각해 볼 때 전공을 정할 때는 적성에 맞는 것을 선택하는 것이 현명한 일인 것 같다.

COMPREHENSION QUESTIONS

1. 한국에서는 왜 모두 입시 준비를 열심히 합니까?
2. 한국의 고등학생들은 대학에 들어가기 위해 어떤 노력을 합니까?
3. 대학에서의 전공은 왜 중요합니까?
4. 어떤 경우 후회할 수도 있습니까?

NEW EXPRESSIONS

1. 대학에 들어가다 'to enter a college'
   대학에 떨어지다 'to fail to enter a college'
   대학을 나오다 'to graduate from college'

2. 재수하다 means 'to study another year' to enter a college.

Notes

CULTURE

대학입시 College entrance exam

한국의 학교 교육은 6년의 초등교육[1], 3년의 중등교육[2], 3년의 고등교육[3], 그리고 4년의 대학 교육으로 이루어져[4] 있다. 대학 입학 시험은 한국 사람들이 가장 스트레스 받는 일 중 하나이다. 대학 입시를 준비하는 고등학생들은 대부분 하루 15시간을 학교에서 보내고, 이 기간[5] 동안 다른 사회 활동[6]은 거의 다 중단된다[7].

한국 사회는 교육을 중요시해[8] 왔다. 조선 시대[9] 남성[10]들은 정부 관료[11]가 되기 위한 과거 시험[12]을 통과하기[13] 위해 노력했는데, 이 전통은 현대사회의 대학 입시에 여전히 남아 있는 것 같다. 한국에는 160여 개의 대학과 전문대학[14]이 있는데, 대학에 입학하기 위한 고등학생들 사이의 경쟁은 매년 아주 치열하다[15].

1. 초등교육: elementary education
2. 중등교육: secondary education
3. 고등교육: higher education
4. 이루어지다: consist of
5. 기간: period (of time)
6. 사회 활동: social activities
7. 중단되다: be ceased
8. 중요시하다: put emphasis on
9. 조선 시대: Joseon dynasty
10. 남성: man, male
11. 정부 관료: government official
12. 과거 시험: *gwageo* exam
13. 통과하다: pass through
14. 전문대학: junior college
15. 치열하다: be intense, fierce

USAGE

1 *Talking about one's major and career goals*

Talking about majors
In pairs, practice the following conversation.

영미: 이번 학기까지 전공을 정해야 되는데 뭐 해야 할지 모르겠어.
수진: 넌 글 쓰는 걸 좋아하잖아. 문학을 전공하는 게 어때?
영미: 응. 나도 작가가 되고 싶긴 한데 부모님이 의대로 갔으면 하시거든.
수진: 그럼 문학을 부전공으로 하는 게 어때?
영미: 좀 힘들지 않을까? 졸업하려면 시간이 많이 걸릴 텐데 . . .
수진: 넌 할 수 있을 거야.

Exercise 1

Interview your partner with the following questions:

(1) 전공을 결정했어요? 전공이 뭐예요?
(2) 어떤 전공이 취직이 잘된다고 생각하세요?
(3) 요즘 가장 인기있는 전공 3가지만 말해 보세요.
(4) 전공을 다시 바꿀 수 있으면 무슨 공부를 해 보고 싶으세요?
(5) 부모님이 원하시는 직업과 자기가 원하는 직업이 다를 때 어떻게 하시겠어요?

Exercise 2

(Role play) You want to be an elementary school teacher, but your parents expect you to apply for medical school. They won't support your educational costs if you take the teaching credentials. Persuade your parents, by emphasizing the positives about being an elementary school teacher.

Talking about careers

In pairs, practice the following dialogue:

(1) 성희: 스티브 씨는 대학 졸업하고 나서 뭐 하고 싶으세요?
스티브: 저는 앞으로 <u>국제 변호사</u>가 되고 싶어요.
성희: 국제 변호사가 되려면 어떻게 준비해야 돼요?
스티브: 대학교를 졸업하고 법대에 가야 됩니다. 또 법대 졸업하고 변호사 시험을 봐서 합격해야 돼요.

(2) 소연: 영진 씨, 뭐 하세요?
영진: 신문 광고 보고 있어요.
소연: 무슨 광고 찾으세요?
영진: 아르바이트 일자리 좀 구하려고요.
소연: 무슨 일자리를 구하세요?
영진: 글쎄요, 은행 직원도 좋고 식당 종업원도 좋을 거 같아요.

Some job titles in Korean

회계사	accountant	의사	doctor
건축가	architect	교육자	educator
예술가	artist	엔지니어	engineer
변호사	attorney	미용사	hairstylist
은행 직원	banker	주부	housekeeper
이발사	barber	간호사	nurse
요리사	chef	물리 치료사	physical therapist
카운슬러	counselor	검사	prosecutor
치과 의사	dentist	비서	secretary
디자이너	designer		

Exercise 1

Change 국제 변호사 in the conversation (1) into other jobs and practice the dialogue again.

Exercise 2

How many more jobs can you list in Korean in addition to the list above?

Exercise 3

Answer the following questions.

(1) 졸업하고 나서 어떤 직장에서 일하고 싶으세요?
(2) 어떤 직장이 좋은 직장이라고 생각하세요?
(3) 좋은 직장을 구하려면 어떻게 해야 돼요?
(4) 직장을 구하려고 면접을 해 본 적이 있으세요?
(5) 면접을 잘하려면 어떻게 준비해야 됩니까?

Exercise 4

Describe the perfect job you want.

2 *Expressing encouragement*

The following expressions are commonly used to encourage other people:

잘되실 거예요.	Everything will be fine.
너무 걱정하시지 마세요.	Don't worry too much.
용기를 내세요./힘내세요.	Cheer up. (용기 'courage')
그냥 해 보세요.	Just try it.
안됐네요.	I'm sorry to hear it.
너무 실망하시지 마세요.	Don't be too disappointed.

Exercise 1

Practice the following dialogues:

(1) A: 운전 시험에 또 떨어졌어요. I failed the driving test again.
B: 저런! 너무 실망하지 마세요.
다음엔 꼭 될 거예요.

(2) A: 어젯밤 머리가 심하게 아파서 한 시간도 못 잤어요.
B: 안됐네요. 오늘은 푹 쉬어 보세요.

(3) A: 라스베가스에 가서 돈을 다 잃어 버렸어요. I lost all my money in Las Vegas.
B: 저런! (쯔쯧!) 너무 실망하지 마세요.
돈이 인생의 전부가 아니잖아요.

(4) A: 방송국 기자 시험을 봤는데 미역국 먹었어요.
B: 힘내세요.

Exercise 2

How would you respond when you hear the following situations from friends?

(1) 취직 시험에 떨어졌어요.
(2) 감기에 걸려서 시험 공부를 하나도 못 했어요.
(3) 할아버지께서 돌아가셨어요.
(4) 아버지 새 차를 몰래 운전하다가 차사고를 냈어요. (몰래 'secretly')
(5) 이가 몹시 아픈데 오늘 일요일이라서 치과가 문을 닫았어요.
(6) 아침에 학교에 오다가 교통 위반 티켓(traffic violation ticket)을 받았어요.
(7) 2년 동안 사귄 남자친구/여자친구하고 헤어졌어요.

3 *Reading ads for jobs*

Read the following ads for jobs.

직원 모집:	방송국 사원 모집:
비서	모집 부문: 비서 & 어카운팅
컴퓨터 기술 필요	3년 이상 경험 있는 사람
경험자 우대	대학에서 어카운팅 전공하신 분.
(213) 441–9861	연락처 (213) 437–2300

Useful expressions

경험자	an experienced person	우대	preference
		연락처	contact number

Exercise 1

Referring to the ads above, call and find out more information about each job. Inquire about the following issues:

(1) salary and benefits
(2) work schedule
(3) holiday and vacation time
(4) travel requirements
(5) interview schedule

Sample dialogue

A: 여보세요. 거기 병원이지요?
B: 네, 그렇습니다.
A: 신문에 난 광고 보고 전화하는데요.
월급은 어떻게 됩니까?
B: 일 년에 4만5천불입니다. 경험 있으세요?

A: 네, 2년 정도 병원에서 일했어요.
B: 밤에도 일하실 수 있으세요?
A: 밤에는 곤란한데요.
B: 주말에는 일하실 수 있으세요?
A: 토요일 오전에는 괜찮아요.
B: 다음 주 화요일 오전 10시에 면접하러 오실 수 있으세요?
A: 네. 거기 주소 좀 알려 주세요.

Exercise 2

You are reading the newspaper want ads. Tell your friend about the ads.

구인 광고

중학교 1학년 학생을
가르칠 가정 교사 구함.
영어, 한국어 이중언어
구사자 원함.
(213) 301-8901

아르바이트 학생 구함.
미술 전공 학생
자기 소개서 지참
영어 필수
월-금 8:30-2:00 시간당 15불
(220) 890-6783

Useful vocabulary

구인	help wanted	지참	bring
이중언어 구사자	bilingual	필수	required
자기 소개서	self-introduction		

Exercise 3

You are interviewing for the jobs described above. Ask four questions about each job.

Lesson 14. Majors and Jobs

CONVERSATION 1 *I'm Worried I'm Going to Mess Up*

Minho: Soyeon, where are you going?
Soyeon: I'm on my way to the broadcast station for an interview to be a broadcaster.
Minho: Oh really? Then you passed the written test! Congratulations!
Soyeon: Thank you.
Minho: I heard that getting hired at a broadcasting station is like trying to pluck a star from the sky.
Soyeon: Yes, they only picked a few people as soon as the announcement came out, but I heard over 500 people applied.
Minho: Really? It's very competitive.
Soyeon: But I'm really worried I'll mess up in the interview today.
Minho: Well you passed the written exam and you're well suited to be a reporter, so I think you'll definitely get the job.
Soyeon: I really hope so.

CONVERSATION 2 *I Would Like to Do Work Related to Economics*

Soyeon enters the interview room and sits down.

Interviewer 1: Please introduce yourself briefly.
Soyeon: My name is Choi Soyeon, and I am a senior majoring in economics at Hankook University. I am currently working as a newspaper reporter at my school.
Interviewer 2: Good. Why did you apply at our broadcast station?
Soyeon: I was very impressed by the news and current affairs programs from this station.
Interviewer 1: Have you given any thought to what field you would like to work in if you become a reporter?
Soyeon: Since my major is economics, I would like to work related to that.
Interviewer 2: Do you think being a reporter suits you?
Soyeon: I think I'll be able to do reporter work well because I really like writing and I'm minoring in literature.
Interviewer 2: Alright.

NARRATION *College in Korea*

Entering college in Korea is very important. People think that getting a good job requires you to graduate from college. So high schoolers study very hard in order to prepare for college entrance exams. Consequently, high school life has become a preparation course for entering college. Korean high schoolers also attend academies outside of school that they study at. There are even some students who fail their entrance exam and continue studying to try again the following year.

When entering college, most students are concerned with what major they will choose. That's because their lives can change drastically based on what major they select. However, in the case that they choose a major based solely on benefits, while ignoring their aptitude for it, they could wind up regretting the decision later. This is because doing a job that doesn't suit you is as uncomfortable as wearing shoes that don't fit. Taking this into consideration, it seems wise to choose a major that matches who you are.

CULTURE *College Entrance Exam*

Korean education consists of 6 years of elementary school, 3 years of middle school, 3 years of high school, and 4 years of college. The college entrance exams are among one of the largest sources of stress for Korean people. Most high school students who are preparing for the college entrance exams spend 15 hours per day at school, and during this period cease almost all social activities.

Korean society was built with an emphasis on education. During the Joseon dynasty, men would work hard to pass the *gwageo* exam in order to become government officials; this tradition seems to be ever lingering in the college entrance exams of modern society. In Korea there are more than 160 universities and junior colleges, and every year the competition between high schoolers to enter these colleges is very fierce.

Grammar Index

Item	Meaning	Lesson
~거나	or	Lesson 11 C2
~거든요	you see (because)	Lesson 4 C1
~게 되다	turn out that	Lesson 3 C1
~게 하다	to make someone/ something . . .	Lesson 9 C1
~구나	speaker's new discovery	Lesson 12 C2
~기가 쉽다/어렵다	it is easy/difficult to . . .	Lesson 2 C1
~기도 하다	sometimes . . . too	Lesson 10 C2
~기는 ~하다	did . . . , but	Lesson 11 C1
~기로 하다	decided to	Lesson 6 C1
~느라고	because of ~ing	Lesson 8 C2
~는 길이다	(be) on one's way	Lesson 4 C1
~는/ㄴ다	plain speech style	Lesson 6 C1
	plain style in speaking	Lesson 6 C1
~는/(으)ㄴ 줄 알다/모르다	know/don't know	Lesson 8 C2
~다가	movement from one action/ state to another	Lesson 5 C2
~다/라/자/냐고 하다	indirect quotation	Lesson 6 C2
~다면서/라면서	confirming information	Lesson 14 C1
~대요/래요	hearsay	Lesson 11 C2
~더라고요	speaker's past experience	Lesson 10 C1
~던	used to	Lesson 1 C2
~아/야	vocative suffix	Lesson 5 C1
아무리 ~어/아도	no matter how	Lesson 6 C2
~어/아	intimate speech style	Lesson 5 C1
~어/아 가지고	because; by doing	Lesson 7 C2
~어/아 보이다	to appear, look	Lesson 7 C1
~어/아 본 적(이) 있다/없다	expresses past experience	Lesson 3 C2
~어/아 버리다	do completely	Lesson 10 C2
~어/아 있다	to be in the state of	Lesson 7 C1
~어/아 죽겠다	. . . to death	Lesson 10 C2
~어/아도 되다	expresses permission	Lesson 2 C2
~(으)ㄴ/는지 알다/ 모르다.	do not know . . . to	Lesson 5 C1

Item	Meaning	Lesson
~어/아야지요	expresses obligation	Lesson 4 C2
~어/아지다	to become	Lesson 1 C1
~었/았다(가)	expressing change in momentum	Lesson 10 C1
~었/았더니	I did . . . and then	Lesson 13 C2
~었/았으면 하다	wish . . . ~ed	Lesson 14 C2
~었었/았었/ㅆ었	remote past	Lesson 3 C2
~(으)ㄴ가보다/나보다	It seems/I guess	Lesson 11 C1
~(으)ㄴ 가요/나요?	Is it (the case) . . .	Lesson 12 C1
~(으)ㄴ/는 거예요/거야	the fact is	Lesson 9 C2
~(으)ㄴ/는/(으)ㄹ 것 같다	it seems like	Lesson 2 C2
~(으)ㄴ/는데도	despite the fact that	Lesson 13 C1
~(으)ㄴ/는 데(에)	in/for ~ing	Lesson 7 C2
~(으)ㄴ/는/(으)ㄹ지	wondering about	Lesson 14 C2
~(으)ㄴ/는 지 [time] 되다	it has been [TIME SPAN] since	Lesson 5 C2
~(으)ㄴ/는 편이다	to tend to	Lesson 5 C1
~(으)ㄴ/는지 알다/모르다	to know/not know whether	Lesson 5 C1
~(으)니까	expresses reason	Lesson 3 C2
~(으)ㄹ 걸 그랬어요	expressing regret	Lesson 12 C1
~(으)ㄹ때	when	Lesson 1 C2
~(으)ㄹ까봐	for fear that	Lesson 14 C1
~(으)ㄹ 뻔하다	almost happened	Lesson 13 C2
~(으)ㄹ 테니까	as (I) intend/expect	Lesson 8 C1
~(으)려고 하다	intend to	Lesson 2 C1
~(으)려다가	about to but then	Lesson 12 C2
~(으)려면	if . . . intends to	Lesson 4 C2
~(으)면 되다	all one needs is	Lesson 3 C1
~(으)면 ~(으)ㄹ 수록	the more . . . the more	Lesson 13 C1
~(으)면 좋겠다	I wish	Lesson 1 C2
~(이)라면	if it were	Lesson 11 C2
(이)든지	any . . .	Lesson 12 C2
~자마자	as soon as	Lesson 14 C1
~잖아요	you know	Lesson 1 C1
~지?	indirect question	Lesson 8 C1
N(이)요	It is a noun	Lesson 4 C2

Korean-English Glossary

2박3일	two nights three days
1학년	freshman
2학년	sophomore
3학년	junior
4학년	senior
가	subject particle
가게	store
가격	price
가구	furniture
가구점	furniture store
가깝다	to be close, near
가끔	sometimes
가끔씩	once in a while
가능하다	be possible
가다	to go
가르치다	to teach
가방	bag
가볍다	to be light
가수	singer
가운데	the middle, the center
가위, 바위, 보	rock-paper-scissors
가을	autumn, fall
가장	the most
가져가다	to take, carry
가족	family
각	each
간장	soy sauce
간판	store signs
감기다	to wash someone's hair
감다	to wash (hair)
감상	appreciation
감상하다	to appreciate
감초	licorice
갈비	*kalbi* (spareribs)
갈아 입다	to change (clothes)
갈아 타다	to change (vehicles)
감기에 걸리다	to have/catch a cold
감사하다	to be thankful
감자	potato
갑자기	suddenly
값	price
강원	Gangwon region
강하다	be strong
갖고 가다	to take
갖고 다니다	to carry around
갖고 오다	to bring
갖다 놓다	to bring and put down somewhere
갖다 드리다*hum.*	to bring/take something to someone
갖다 주다*plain*	to bring/take something to someone
같이	1. together; 2. like, as
개	1. dog; 2. item (counter)
개월	month
걔	that kid
거	thing (contraction of 것)
거기	there
거리	1. distance; 2. street, avenue
거스름돈	change (money)
거실	living room
거의	almost
거품	bubble
걱정	worry, concern
걱정하다	to worry
건강하다	to be healthy
건너다	to cross
건너편	the other side
건드리다	to touch
건물	building
건조하다	to be dry
건축물	building, structure
건축학	architecture
걷다	to walk
걸다	to call
걸리다	to take [time]
걸어가다	to go on foot
걸어다니다	to walk around
걸어오다	to come on foot
검정색	black
것	thing (=거)
게임	game
겨우	barely
겨울	winter
결혼	marriage
결혼식	wedding
결혼식장	wedding hall

결혼하다	to get married
겹치다	to overlap
경기	match, game
경기장	sports stadium
경우	case
경쟁	competition
경쟁하다	to compete
경제학	economics
경주	Gyeongju
경찰	police
경찰서	police station
경치	scenery, view
경험	experience
경험하다	to experience
계단	stairs
계란	egg
계산서	check
계속	continuously
계속되다	to continue
계시다*hon.*	to be (existence), stay
계절	season
계절 학기	summer/winter term
계좌	account
계획	plan
계획하다	to plan
고3	high school senior
고기	meat
고등교육	higher education
고등학교	high school
고등학생	high school student
고르다	to choose, select
고맙다	to be thankful
고민	worry
고민하다	to worry
고생	hardship
고생하다	to have a difficult time
고속도로	highway, freeway
고장	breakdown
고장나다	to break down
고추장	red-pepper paste
고층빌딩	high-rise building
고향	hometown
곧	right away, soon
골동품	antique
골프	golf
곳	place
곳곳	everywhere
공	0 (zero: for phone #)
공기	air
공부	study
공부방	study room
공부하다	to study
공사	construction
공예품	craftwork
공원	park
공장	factory
공짜	free
공포 영화	horror movie
공항	airport
과	1. lesson, chapter; 2. and (joins nouns)
과거 시험	*gwageo* exam
과목	course, subject
과일	fruit
과자	cracker
과정	process
과제	assignment
과학	science
관계	relationship
관련	relation, connection
관련되다	be related
관심	interest, concern
관악산	Gwanak Mountain
괜찮다	to be all right, okay
굉장히	very much
교과서	textbook
교복	school uniform
교수님	professor
교실	classroom
교육학	education, pedagogy
교통	traffic
교통 표지판	traffic sign
교통카드	transportation card
교회	church
구경	sightseeing
구경하다	to look around; to sightsee
구두	dress shoes
구두 시험	oral exam
구름	cloud
구름이 끼다	to get cloudy
구하다	to search for
국	soup
국가적	national
국경일	national holidays
국내선	domestic flight
국물	soup, broth
국제선	international flight 국제
전화	international call
군데	place, spot

굵다	be thick
굽	heel
궁금하다	be curious
권	volume (counter)
귀걸이	earring
귀찮다	be troublesome
규칙	regulations
규칙적	regular
규칙적이다	be regular
귤	tangerine
그	that
그냥	just, without any special reason
그동안	meantime
그래서	so, therefore
그램	gram
그러고 보니	come to think of it
그러니까	so
그러면	then, in that case
그런데	1. but, however; 2. by the way
그럼	(if so) then
그렇다	to be so
그렇지만	but, however
그릇	plate, bowl
그리고	and
그리다	to draw
그림	picture, painting
그립다	to miss, long for
그만	without doing anything further
극장	movie theater
근처	nearby, vicinity
글쎄요	Well; It's hard to say
금반지	gold ring
금방	soon
금요일	Friday
급하다	be urgent
기간	period (of time)
기계 공학	mechanical engineering
기다려지다	to be wished
기다리다	to wait
기분	feeling
기쁘다	to be joyful, glad
기사	driver
기숙사	dormitory
기억	memory
기억나다	to remember
기억하다	to remember
기온	temperature
기원전	B.C.
기원하다	to wish
기자	reporter
기준	standard
기차	train
기침	cough
기침하다	to cough
기타	guitar
길	1. street, road ; 2. way
길다	to be long
길러내다	to train, raise
김밥	*kimbap*
김치	kimchi
깊다	to be deep
까만색	black (=까망)
까맣다	to be black
까지	1. up to (location); 2. to/until/through (time); 3. including
깎다	1. to cut down; 2. to cut (hair)
깔다	to spread
깜빡	with a flash
깨끗하다	to be clean
깨다	1. to wake up; 2. to break
깨우다	to wake someone up
깨지다	to break
께*hon.*	to (a person)
께서*hon.*	subject particle (=이/가 *plain*)
꺼내다	to take out
꼭	surely, certainly
꽃	flower
꽃집	flower shop
꽉	tightly, fully
꿈(을) 꾸다	to dream a dream
끄다	to turn off
끓이다	to boil
끝나다	to be over, finished
끝내다	to end
끼다	to be foggy
끼다	to wear (glasses, gloves, rings)
나*plain*	I (=저*hum.*)
나가다	to go out
나누다	to share
나다	happen, break out

나라	country
나쁘다	to be bad
나오다	to come out
나이	age
나이가 들다	to gain age
나중에	later
나타내다	to show, represent
나흘	four days
난방	heating
날	day
날마다	everyday
날씨	weather
날씬하다	to be slim
날짜	date
남	south
남기다	to leave (a message)
남녀	men and women
남다	to remain
남동생	younger brother
남미	South America
남부	southern
남산	Nam Mountain
남색	navy blue, indigo
남성	man, male
남아있다	to remain
남자	man
남편	husband
낫다	to recover
낮	daytime
낮다	to be low
낮아지다	to get lower
낮잠	nap
내*plain*	my (=제*hum.*)
내년	next year
내다	1. to pay (money); 2. to turn in (homework); 3. to make time
내려가다	to go down
내리다	to get off
내일	tomorrow
냄새	smell
냄새 나다	to smell
냉면	*naengmyŏn* (cold buckwheat noodles)
냉장고	refrigerator
너	you (*plain*)
너무	too much
넓다	to be spacious, wide
넘다	to exceed
넘어지다	to fall (down)
넣다	to put in
네	1. yes; 2. I see; 3. okay
네거리	intersection
넥타이	necktie
년	year (counter)
노란색	yellow
노랗다	to be yellow
노래	song
노래 부르다	to sing
노래하다	to sing
노래방	karaoke room
녹용	deer antler
녹음	recording
녹음하다	to record
녹차	green tea
논문	thesis
놀다	1. to play; 2. to not work
놀라다	to be startled
놀러가다	to go on an outing
놀러오다	to come around
놀이공원	amusement park
농구	basketball
농구하다	to play basketball
농구 시합	basketball game
농담	joke
농사	farming
높다	to be high
놓아 주다	to put something down for someone
놓치다	to miss, lose
누가	1. who (누구+가); 2. someone
누구	1. who; 2. someone
누나	the older sister of a male
누르다	to press, push
눈(이) 오다	to snow
눈	1. eyes; 2. snow
눕다	to lie down
뉴스	news
뉴욕	New York
느낌	feeling, sense
늘다	to increase
는	topic particle ('as for')

늘다 to improve
늦게 late
늦다 to be late
늦잠 oversleep
님 honorific noun suffix
다 all
다녀 오다 to go and get back
다니다 1. to attend;
2. to get around
다듬다 to trim
다르다 to be different
다보탑 Dabo Tower
다소 more or less; to some degree
다시 again
다리 leg
다양하다 to be diverse
다음 next, following
다음부터(는) from next time
다이어트 diet
다치다 to hurt
다행이다 be fortunate, relief
다행히 fortunately
단 bundle; bunch
단어 vocabulary
단오 Dano day
단정하다 to be neat
단풍 fall foliage
담다 to put something into something
닫다 to close
닫히다 to be closed
달 1. month (counter);
2. moon
달구다 to heat
달다 to be sweet
달러 dollar (=불)
달력 calendar
닮다 to resemble
담배 cigarette
답 answer
답장 reply
답장하다 to reply
닷새 five days
당근 carrot
당연히 of course, naturally
당황하다 be flustered
대답 answer
대답하다 to answer
대문 gate
대부분 mostly
대신 intead of
대접하다 to treat, serve
대중 the public
대체로 generally, mostly
대충 roughly
대통령 president
대통령 선거 presidential election
대학 college, university
대학교 college, university
대학생 college student
대학원 graduate school
대학원생 graduate student
대한항공 Korean Air
대해서 about
댁*hon.* home, house (=집*plain*)
더 more
더럽다 to be dirty
덜 less
덥다 to be hot
덮다 to close, cover
데 place
데이트 a date
데이트하다 to date
도 1. also, too;
2. degree
도둑 thief
도서관 library
도시 city
도와 드리다*hon.* to help
도와 주다*plain* to help
도움 help
도착하다 to arrive
도쿄 Tokyo
독감 flu
독방 single room
독서 reading
독서하다 to read
돈 money
돈을 내다 to pay
돈을 벌다 to earn money
돈이 들다 to cost money
돌 the first birthday
돌다 to turn
돌려 드리다*hum.* to return (something to someone)
돌려 주다*plain* to return (something to someone)
돌리다 to change (the channel)
돌아가다 to return (to)

돌아가시다*hon.*	to pass away
돌아오다	to return, come back
돕다	to help
동	east
동남아	Southeast Asia
동네	neighborhood
동대문시장	Dongdaemun Market
동물원	zoo
동부	East Coast
동생	younger sibling
동아리	(social) club, group
동안	during
동양학	Asian studies
동영상	video, movie file
동창회	alumni
동호회	(amateur) club
되다	1. to become; 2. get, turn into; 3. to function, work
되도록	as . . . as possible
된장찌개	soybean-paste stew
두	two (with counter)
두 번째	the second
두껍다	to be thick
두드리다	to knock, hit
두부	tofu
둘	two
뒤	the back, behind
뒷머리	back hair
드라마	drama
드라이어	hair dryer
드럼	drum
드리다*hum.*	to give (=주다*plain*)
드물다	be rare
드시다*hon.*	to eat (=먹다*plain*)
듣다	1. to listen; 2. to take a course
들	plural particle
들르다	to stop by
들어가다	1. to enter; 2. to get a job/work
들어오다	to come in
들어있다	to contain
등	et cetera
등기	registered (mail)
등산	hiking
등산객	mountain climber
등산하다	to hike
디저트	dessert
따님*hon.*	daughter
따다	to pick, pluck
따뜻하다	to be warm
따라하다	to repeat after
따로	separately
딸	daughter
때	time
때문에	because of
떠나다	to leave
떠들다	to make noise
떡	rice cake
떡국	rice cake soup
떡볶이	spicy rice cake
떨어지다	1. to fall; 2. to be rejected
또	1. and, also, too; 2. again
똑같다	to be identical
똑바로	straight, upright
뚱뚱하다	to be fat
뛰다	to run
뜨겁다	to be hot
뜨다	to rise; to come up
뜻	meaning
뜻하다	to mean, signify
라디오	radio
라면	instant noodles (ramen)
라운지	lounge
램프	lamp
랩	lab
러시아	Russia
런던	London
로스앤젤레스	Los Angeles (L.A.)
록	rock music
롤	roll
룸메이트	roommate
를	object particle
마늘	garlic
마당	yard
마르다	to be skinny
마리	animal (counter)
마사지	massage
마시다	to drink
마을 버스	town shuttle bus
마음	mind, heart
마음씨	mind, heart
마음에 들다	to be to one's liking
마중 나가다	to go out to greet someone

마중 나오다	to come out to greet someone
마지막	last
마치	like, as if
마치다	to finish
마침	just, just in time
마켓	market
마트	discount stores
막내	youngest child
막히다	to be blocked, congested
만	only
만나다	to meet
만드는 법	recipe
만들다	to make
만큼	as . . . as
만화방	comic book rental store
만화책	comic book
많다	to be many, much
많이	much, many
말	speech, words
말고	not N1 but N2
말리다	to dry
말씀*hon.*	speech, words (=말*plain*)
말하다	to speak
맑다	to be clear
맛보다	to taste
맛없다	to be tasteless, not delicious
맛있다	to be delicious
맞다	1. to fit; 2. to be correct
맞추다	to set, adjust
매년	every year
매다	to tie
매달	every month
매일	every day
매주	every week
매표소	ticket office
맵다	to be spicy
머리	1. head; 2. hair
먹거리	things to eat
먹다	1. to eat; 2. to gain age
먹이다	to feed
먼저	first, beforehand
멀다	to be far
멋있다	to be stylish, attractive
메뉴	menu
메시지	message
멕시코	Mexico
며칠	1. what date; 2. a few days
면	noodles
면도	shaving
면도하다	to shave
면접	interview
면접관	interviewer
면접장	interview site
명	people (counter)
명절	traditional holidays
몇	how many, what (with a counter)
모기	mosquito
모두	all
모래	sand
모레	the day after tomorrow
모르다	to not know, be unaware of
모시다 (부모)	to have one's parents with
모양	shape
모으다	to collect
모이다	to gather
모임	gathering
모자	cap, hat
모자라다	to lack
모텔	motel
목	throat
목(이) 마르다	to be thirsty
목걸이	necklace
목도리	muffler, scarf
목소리	voice
목요일	Thursday
목욕	bath
목욕탕	public bathhouse
목욕하다	to bathe
몸	body
몸조리	care of health
못	cannot
못생기다	to be ugly
무겁다	to be heavy
무게	weight
무덥다	to be hot and humid
무료	free of charge
무섭다	to be scary; scared
무스	mousse
무슨	1. what, what kind of; 2. some kind of

무시하다	to ignore
무엇	what (=뭐)
무척	very much
문	door
문명	civilization
문병	visit (someone sick)
문병하다	to visit (someone sick)
문자	text message
문제	problem
문학	literature
문화	culture
묻다	to ask
물	water
물가	cost of living
물건	merchandise, stuff
물다	to bite
물리다	to be bitten
물리학	physics
물어보다	to inquire
물품	articles, goods
뭐	1. what (=무엇); 2. something
미국	the United States
미끄럽다	be slippery
미리	in advance
미안하다	to be sorry
미역국	seaweed soup
미용사	hairstylist
미용실	beauty salon
미인	beautiful woman
미터기	meter
민감하다	be sensitive
민속촌	Folk Village
밑	the bottom, below
바겐 세일	bargain sale
바꾸다	to change, switch
바뀌다	to be changed
바다	sea
바닥	floor
바닷가	beach
바람	wind
바로	directly
바르다	to apply
바빠지다	to get busier
바쁘다	to be busy
바이올린	violin
바지	pants
박물관	museum
박스	box
밖	outside
밖에	nothing but, only
반	1. class; 2. half
반갑다	to be glad
반값	half price
반달	half moon
반대	opposite
반드시	surely, certainly
반말	informal/impolite speech
반면(에)	on the other hand
반바지	shorts
반지	ring
반찬	side dishes
반하다	to fall in love
받다	to receive
발	foot
발달	development
발달시키다	to develop
발달하다	to develop, grow
발매기	vending machine
발음	pronunciation
밝다	to be bright
밤	night
밤새	all night long
밥	1. cooked rice; 2. meal
방	room
방금	a moment ago
방법	method
방송국	broadcasting station
방송되다	be aired
방학	school vacation
배	1. stomach, abdomen; 2. pear
배(가) 고프다	to be hungry
배(가) 부르다	to have a full stomach
배달	delivery
배달하다	to deliver
배우	actor
배우다	to learn
배터리	battery
백만	million
백화점	department store
밴쿠버	Vancouver
버스	bus
번	1. number (counter); 2. number of times (e.g., 한 번)
번영	prosperity

Korean	English
번째	ordinal numbers
번호	number
벌	a pair of (counter)
벌다	to earn (money)
벌레	insect
벌써	already
법대	law school
법학	law
벗기다	to take someone's clothes off
벗다	to take off, undress
벗어나다	get out of
별	star
별로	not really/particularly
별미	gourmet
별일	anything particular
변하다	to change, alter
변화하다	to change
병	disease
병원	hospital
보내다	1. to spend time; 2. to send
보다	to see, look, watch
보다	than
보름	fifteen days
보스톤	Boston
보이다	to be seen, visible
보충하다	to complement
보통	1. usually; 2. regular
복	good fortune
복도	aisle
복습	review
복잡하다	to be crowded
볶다	to stir-fry
본인	oneself
본인 확인	self-identification
볼거리	things to watch
볼링	bowling
볼펜	ballpoint pen
봄	spring
봉지	pack; bag
봉투	envelope
뵙다*hum.*	to see (=보다*plain*)
부러지다	to fracture
부럽다	be envious of
부르다	1. to sing (a song); 2. to call out
부모님	parents
부부	married couple

Korean	English
부분	part
부엌	kitchen
부자	a wealthy person
부전공	minor
부족하다	to be insufficient
부치다	to mail (a letter, parcel)
부탁하다	to ask a favor
부터	from (time) . . .
북	north
분	minute (counter)
분*hon.*	people (=명*plain*)
분야	area
불	1. dollar (=달러); 2. light; fire
불고기	*pulgogi* (roasted meat)
불교	Buddhism
불국사	Pulgugsa
불다	to blow
불리다	be called
불편하다	to be uncomfortable, inconvenient
붐비다	be crowded
붙다	to be accepted
붙이다	to stick, affix
브로드웨이 극장	Broadway theater
블라우스	blouse
비	rain
비(가) 오다	to rain
비교적	relatively
비누	soap
비빔밥	*pibimbap* (rice with vegetables and beef)
비슷하다	to be similar
비싸다	to be expensive
비자	visa
비행기	airplane
빌다	to beg, ask for
빌딩	building
빌려주다	to lend
빌리다	to borrow
빠르다	to be fast
빠지다	to drop/leave out
빨간색	red
빨갛다	to be red
빨래하다	to do the laundry
빨리	fast, quickly
빵	bread
빼앗기다	to be deprived of
뽑다	to single out

사	4
사 먹다	to buy and eat
사거리	intersection
사고	accident
사과	apple
사귀다	1. to make friends; 2. to date
사다	to buy
사람	person, people
사랑	love
사랑하다	to love
사모님	teacher's wife
사무실	office
사실	fact, truth
사업	business
사용하다	to use
사우나	sauna
사이	1. relationship; 2. between
사이즈	size
사인	sign, signature
사전	dictionary
사진	photo, picture
사찰	temple
사투리	dialect
사회	society
사회보장번호	Social Security number
사회 활동	social activities
사흘	three days
살	1. years old; 2. flesh, fat
살다	to live
살리다	to spare, save; to nurture
살림	housekeeping, living
살이 찌다	to gain weight
살짝	slightly
삼	3
삼촌	uncle
상	1. table; 2. award
상가	shopping district
상관없이	regardless of
상다리	table legs
상담	counseling
상대편	opponent
상자	box
상점	store
상징하다	to symbolize
상추	lettuce
상쾌하다	be refreshing
상품	prize; merchandise
상품권	gift certificate
상하다	1. to get damaged; 2. to spoil
상황	situation
새	new
새로	newly
새롭다	be new, original
새벽	dawn
새우다 (밤을)	to stay up all night
새해	New Year
색	color (=색깔)
샌드위치	sandwich
샌들	sandals
생각나다	be reminded
생기다	1. to look like; 2. be formed
생년월일	date of birth
생물학	biology
생선	fish
생신*hon.*	birthday
생일	birthday
생활	daily life, living
샤워	shower
샤워하다	to take a shower
샴페인	champagne
샴푸	shampoo
서	west
서기	A.D.
서다	to stand
서두르다	to hurry
서랍	drawer
서로	each other
서비스	service
서양식	Western style
서양의학	Western medicine
서울	Seoul
서울대입구역	Seoul National University Station
서울타워	Seoul Tower
서점	bookstore (=책방)
서투르다	be unskilled
석가탑	Seokga Tower
석굴암	Seokguram (stone cave)
선물	present, gift
선물하다	to give a present, gift
선생님	teacher
선수	athlete
선택	choice, selection
선택하다	to choose, select

설거지	dishwashing
설거지하다	to wash dishes
설날	New Year's Day
설악산	Seorak Mount
설탕	sugar
섬	island
섭씨	Celsius
성격	personality
성별	sex, gender
성적	grade
성함*hon.*	name (=이름*plain*)
세기	century
세배	New Year's bow
세뱃돈	New Year's cash gift
세수하다	to wash one's face
세우다	to stop, pull over
세일	sale
세제	detergent
세탁기	washing machine
세탁소	laundry, cleaner's
세트	a set
센트	cent
셔츠	shirt
소개	introduction
소개시키다	to introduce someone
소개하다	to introduce
소고기	beef
소극적이다	to be passive
소리	sound, noise
소매	sleeve
소문	rumor
소방서	fire station
소설	novel
소식	news
소원	wish
소통	communication
소통하다	to communicate
소파	sofa
소포	parcel, package
소화	digestion
손	hand
손(을) 씻다	to wash one's hands
손님	guest, customer
손질하다	to fix up
손톱 손질	manicure
솜씨	skill, ability
송편	songpyen
쇼	show
쇼핑	shopping
쇼핑하다	to shop
수고하다	to put forth effort, take trouble
수도	capital city
수선	alteration
수업	course, class
수영	swimming
수영장	swimming pool
수영하다	to swim
수요일	Wednesday
수저	spoon and chopsticks
수프	soup
숙제	homework
숙제하다	to do homework
순간	the moment
순두부찌개	soft tofu stew
순서	order, turn
숟가락	spoon
술	alcoholic beverage
술집	pub, bar
숫자	number
쉬다	to rest
쉽다	to be easy
슈퍼(마켓)	supermarket
스릴러	thriller
스시	sushi
스웨터	sweater
스키	ski
스키 타다	to ski
스타일	style
스트레스	stress
스파게티	spaghetti
스페인	Spain
스포츠	sports
슬리퍼	slipper
슬프다	to be sad
승차권	ride pass, ticket
시	hour, o'clock
시간	time, hour (duration)
시간이 흐르면서	over time
시계	clock, watch
시금치	spinach
시끄럽다	to be noisy
시내	downtown
시다	to be sour
시대	period
시드니	Sydney
시사	current affairs
시원하다	to be cool, refreshing
시원해지다	to become cooler

시작하다	to begin
시장	marketplace
시청	city hall
시청역	city hall station
시카고	Chicago
시키다	to order (food)
시합	game, match
시험	test, exam
식구	family member
식당	restaurant
식비	food expenses
식사	meal
식사하다	to have a meal
식성	appetite
식탁	dining table
식후	after a meal
신기다	to put (footwear) on someone
신기하다	to be amazing
신나다	to be excited
신다	to wear (footwear)
신라	Silla
신랑	groom
신문	newspaper
신문사	newspaper publisher
신발	shoes
신부	bride
신분증	identification card
신용 카드	credit card
신체부위	body parts
신체특성	body character
신호등	traffic light
신혼부부	newlywed couple
신혼여행	honeymoon
실	thread
실력	skill, ability
실례하다	to be excused
실수	mistake
실수하다	to make a mistake
싫다	to be undesirable
싫어하다	to dislike
심리학	psychology
심심하다	to be bored
심하다	be severe
싱겁다	to be bland
싶다	to want to
싸다	1. to be cheap; 2. to wrap; 3. to pack
싸우다	to fight

쌓이다	to be piled up
썰다	to slice
쑥	mugwort
쓰다	1. to write; 2. to use; 3. to wear headgear; 4. to be bitter
쓰러지다	to collapse
쓰이다	to be used
씨	attached to a person's name for courtesy
씩	each, apiece
씨름	Korean wrestling
아	oh
아기	baby
아까	a while ago
아내	wife
아니다	to not be (negative equation)
아니요	no
아들	son
아래층	downstairs
아르바이트	part-time job
아름답다	to be beautiful
아마	probably, perhaps
아무	any
아무거나	anything
아무리	no matter how
아버지	father
아쉽다	to be sad, feel the lack of
아시아	Asia
아이	child
아이고	oh my
아이스크림	ice cream
아이스하키	ice hockey
아저씨	mister; a man of one's parents' age
아주	very, really
아주머니	middle-aged woman
아직	yet, still
아직도	yet, still
아침	1. breakfast; 2. morning
아파트	apartment
아프다	to be sick
악기	musical instrument
안	1. the inside; 2. do not
안개	fog
안경	eyeglasses

안녕하다	to be well
안녕히	in peace
안방	master bedroom
안부	regards
안전 벨트	seat belt
안전하다	to be safe
앉다	to sit
않다	to not be, to not do
알다	to know
알래스카	Alaska
알리다	to inform
알아듣다	to understand, recognize
알아보다	to find out, check out
앞	the front
액세서리	accessory
액션	action
야구	baseball
야구공	baseball
야구하다	to play baseball
야구장	baseball stadium
야외	the outside
야채	vegetable
약	1. approximately; 2. medicine
약간	slightly
약국	drugstore
약도	map
약사	pharmacist
약속	1. engagement; 2. promise
약재	medicinal ingredients
알	pills (counter)
얇게	thinly
얇다	to be thin
양	quantity
양념	condiment, seasoning
양념하다	to season
양력	solar calendar
양말	socks, stockings
양식	Western-style (food)
양파	onion
양측	both parties
앞	the front
앞두다	to have something ahead
앞머리	bangs
앞으로	in the future
얘기	talk, chat (=이야기)
얘기하다	to talk, chat
어	oh
어느	which
어둡다	to be dark
어떤	which, what kind of
어떻게	how
어떻다	to be how
어디	1. what place, where; 2. somewhere
어렵다	to be difficult
어른	adult, (one's) elders
어리다	to be young
어린이	child
어머	Oh! Oh my! Dear me!
어머니	mother
어서	quick(ly)
어업	fishery
어울리다	to match, suit
어제	yesterday
어젯밤	last night
어치	worth, value
언니	the older sister of a female
언어학	linguistics
언제	1. when; 2. sometime
언제나	all the time
얹다	to put
얻다	to gain
얼굴	face
얼다	to freeze
얼마	1. how long/much; 2. some (time, amount)
얼마나	how long/much
얼음	ice
엄마	mom
없다	1. to not be (existence); 2. to not have
없어지다	to disappear
에	1. in, at, on (static location); 2. to (destination); 3. at, in, on (time); 4. for, per
에 따라	according to
에서	1. in, at (dynamic location); 2. from (location); 3. from (time)
에어컨	air-conditioner
엘리베이터	elevator

여가	free time
여권	passport
여기	here
여동생	younger sister
여러	many, several
여름	summer
여보	honey, dear
여보세요	hello (on the phone)
여자	woman
여자 친구	girlfriend
여전히	still, as ever
여태	still, so far yet
여행	travel, trip
여행사	travel agency
여행하다	to travel
역	station
역사	history
역할	role
연결	connection, link
연결하다	to connect, link
연구실	professor's office
연극	play, drama
연락	contact
연락하다	to contact
연령대	age group
연세*hon.*	age (=나이*plain*)
연습	practice
연습 문제	exercise
연습하다	to practice
연애	dating
연애하다	to date
연주	musical performance
연주하다	to perform on a musical instrument
연필	pencil
연휴	long weekend
열	fever
열다	to open
열리다	to be open
열쇠	key
열심히	diligently
열흘	ten days
엽서	postcard
영	0 (zero)
영국	the United Kingdom
영서	Yeongseo region
영수증	receipt
영어	the English language
영업	business
영하	below the freezing point
영화	movie
옆	the side, beside
옆머리	the side of the head
예	yes, I see, okay (=네)
예능	entertainment
예를 들어	for example
예쁘다	to be pretty
예술	art
예식장	wedding hall
예약	reservation
예약하다	to reserve
예전	old days
옛날	the old days
오늘	today
오다	to come
오래	long time
오래간만	after a long time
오랫동안	for a long time
오른쪽	right side
오빠	the older brother of a female
오전	a.m.
오페라	opera
오후	afternoon
온돌	floor heating system
올라가다	to go up
올리다	to post up
올림	sincerely yours
올림픽	Olympics
올해	this year
옮기다	to move, shift
옷	clothes
옷가게	clothing store
옷장	wardrobe, closet
와	1. and (joins nouns); 2. Wow!
와이셔츠	dress shirt
완전히	completely
왕복	round trip
왜	why
왜냐하면	because, since
외국	foreign country
외국어	foreign language
외국인	foreigner
외국인등록번호	Alien Registration Number
외롭다	to be lonely
외식하다	to eat out
외우다	to memorize
왼쪽	left side

요금	fee, fare
요리	cooking
요리하다	to cook
요새	these days
요즘	these days
우리*plain*	we/us/our (=저희*hum.*)
우산	umbrella
우승자	the winner
우연히	by chance, accident
우유	milk
우체국	post office
우체부	postman
우체통	postbox
우편	mail service
우편 번호	postal code
우편 요금	postage
우표	stamp
운	luck, fortune
운동	exercise
운동장	playground
운동하다	to exercise
운동화	sports shoes, sneakers
운세	fortune
운전	driving
운전 면허	driver's license
운전하다	to drive
울다	to cry
울리다	to make someone cry
웃기다	to make someone laugh
웃다	to laugh
원 (₩)	won (Korean currency)
원룸	studio apartment
원피스	(one-piece) dress
원하다	to wish, want
월	month (counter)
월급	salary
월드컵	World Cup
월요일	Monday
웨딩드레스	wedding gown
웬만하면	if possible
웬일	what's up
위	1. the top side, above; 2. stomach
위치	location
위하다	to care for
위한	for, in order to
위험하다	to be dangerous
유난히	particularly
유니온 빌딩	Union Building
유니폼	uniform
유럽	Europe
유명하다	to be famous
유일한	one and only
유학생	student abroad
유행	fashion, trend
유행하다	to be in fashion
육개장	hot shredded-beef soup
윷놀이	yut game
으로	1. by means of; 2. toward, to; 3. item selected among many other options
은	topic particle ('as for')
은행	bank
을	object particle
음력	lunar calendar
음료수	beverage
음식	food
음식값	food cost
음식점	restaurant (=식당)
음악	music
음악회	concert
응	yeah
의	of
의견	opinion
의대	medical school
의미	meaning
의미하다	to signify
의사	doctor
의생활	clothing habits
의자	chair
의학기술	medical technology
이(를) 닦다	to brush one's teeth
이	1. 2; 2. subject particle; 3. this; 4. a suffix inserted after a Korean first name that ends in a consonant; 5. tooth
이거	this (=이것)
이기다	to win
이다	to be (equation)
이따가	a little later
이렇게	like this, this way
이름	name
이루어지다	consist of

이르다	be early
이메일	e-mail
이발	haircut (for men)
이발사	barber
이발소	barbershop
이발하다	to get a haircut (for men)
이번	this time
이사하다	to move
이상	abnormality
이상하다	be strange, odd
이스트 홀	East Hall
이야기	talk, chat (=얘기)
이야기하다	to talk (=얘기하다)
이용하다	to utilize
이웃	neighbor, neighborhood
이젠	now (이제+는)
이쪽으로	this way + 으로
이태리	Italy
이틀	two days
이해하다	to understand
익숙하다	to be familiar
인간	human being
인구	population
인기	popularity
인도	sidewalk
인사	greeting
인사하다	to greet
인사동	Insadong
인사하다	to greet
인삼	ginseng
인상적	memorable
인생	(human) life
인연	tie, connection (people)
인천	Incheon
인터넷	Internet
인터뷰	interview
일 인분	one portion
일	1. 1; 2. day (counter); 3. work; 4. event
일기	journal
일기예보	weather forecast
일등석	first-class seat
일반석	economy-class seat
일본	Japan
일부분	one part
일식	Japanese food
일어나다	to get up
일어서다	to stand up
일요일	Sunday
일찍	early
일하다	to work
읽다	to read
잃어버리다	to lose
입구	entrance
입다	to wear, put on (clothes)
입시	entrance exam
입원	hospitalization
입원하다	to hospitalize
입학	school admission
입학하다	to enter a school
입히다	to dress someone
있다	1. to be (existence); 2. to have
잊다	to forget
잊어버리다	to forget
자기 소개	self-introduction
자녀	children, offspring
자다	to sleep
자동 응답기	answering machine
자동차	automobile
자라다	to grow up
자랑하다	to boast
자르다	to cut
자리	1. seat; 2. digit
자연	nature
자연스럽다	be natural
자전거	bicycle
자주	often, frequently
자취	living on one's own
자취하다	to live on one's own
자켓	jacket
작가	writer
작년	last year
작다	to be small (in size)
잔	glass, cup
잔치	feast, party
잘	well
잘라 드리다*hum.*	to cut (something for someone)
잘라 주다*plain*	to cut (something for someone)
잘못하다	to do wrong
잘생기다	to be handsome
잠	sleep
잠깐만	for a short time
잠들다	to fall asleep
잠시	briefly

잠실 Jamsil
잠을 자다 to sleep
잠이 들다 to fall asleep
잡다 to catch, grab
잡지 magazine
잡채 *japchae*
잡히다 to be caught
장(을) 보다 to buy one's groceries
장갑 gloves
장거리 전화 long-distance call
장남 first son
장롱 closet
장마 rainy season
장만하다 to purchase, get
장소 place, location
장수 long life
장수하다 to live a long life
장학금 scholarship
장화 boots
재미없다 to be uninteresting
재미있다 to be interesting, fun
재료 ingredient, material
재수 retaking the college entrance exam
재수하다 to retake the college entrance exam
재우다 to get someone to sleep
재즈 jazz
재학 중 be in school
저 that (over there)
저*hum.* I (=나*plain*)
저기 over there
저녁 1. evening; 2. dinner
저어 uh (expression of hesitation)
저절로 automatically
저희*hum.* we/us/our (=우리*plain*)
적극적이다 to be positive
적다 1. to be few, scarce; 2. to write down
적당하다 be adequate
적성 aptitude
적어도 at least
적응 adaptation
적응하다 to adapt
적절하다 be adequate
전 before
전공 major
전공하다 to major
전국 the whole nation
전기공학 electrical engineering
전문 one's specialty
전문대학 junior college
전부 all together
전세계 the whole world
전통 tradition
전통 문화 traditional culture
전통 찻집 traditional teahouse
전하다 to tell, convey
전혀 not at all
전화 telephone
전화번호 telephone number
전화비 telephone bill
전화하다 to make a telephone call
절 Buddhist temple
절대 never
젊다 be young
점 point, aspect
점술인 fortune-teller
점심 lunch
점원 clerk, salesperson
점점 gradually
점퍼 jumper/jacket
접시 plate
젓가락 chopsticks
정 affection
정가 regular price
정도 approximate
정류장 (bus) stop
정리 arrangement
정리하다 to arrange, organize
정말 really
정보 information
정부 관료 government official
정신없다 be mindless
정원 yard, garden
정육점 butcher shop
정장 suit, formal dress
정치학 political science
정하다 to decide, set
정확하다 to be accurate
제*hum.* my (=내*plain*)
제과점 bakery
제대로 properly
제일 first, most
제주도 Jeju Island
조건 condition
조그맣다 to be small
조금 a little (=좀)

조상	ancestor
조선시대	Joseon dynasty
조심하다	to be careful
조용하다	to be quiet
졸다	to doze off
졸리다	to be sleepy
졸업	graduation
졸업하다	to graduate
졸업식	commencement
좀	a little (contraction of 조금)
좁다	to be narrow
종업원	employee
종이	paper
좋다	to be good, nice
좋아하다	to like
좌석	seat
죄송하다	to be sorry
주	week
주다	to give
주로	mostly, mainly
주말	weekend
주무시다*hon.*	to sleep (=자다*plain*)
주문하다	to order
주민등록번호	Resident Registration number
주민등록증	Resident Registration card
주소	address
주스	juice
주유소	gas station
주인	owner
주인공	main character
주차장	parking lot
죽다	to die
준비	preparation
준비하다	to prepare
줄이다	to shorten, decrease
중간	the middle
중고 가구	used furniture
중고품	used merchandise
중국	China
중단되다	be ceased
중대사	serious matter
중등교육	secondary education
중매	matchmaking
중부 지방	the central districts
중시하다	put emphasis on
중식	Chinese food
중심지	the pivot, center
중앙 우체국	Central Post Office
중에서	between, among
중요하다	to be important
중학교	middle school
중학생	middle school student
즉	that is
즐겁다	to be joyful
즐기다	to enjoy
증상	symptom
증진시키다	to increase
지각	lateness
지각하다	to be late
지갑	wallet
지겹다	to be boring
지금	now
지나가다	to pass by
지나다	to pass, go by
지난	last, past
지내다	1. to get along; 2. to have (a ceremony)
지다	1. to lose; 2. to go down (the Sun)
지도	map
지방	region, district
지속적으로	consistently
지역 번호	area code
지원하다	to apply
지정하다	to appoint
지키다	to guard, protect
지하도	underpass
지하 상가	underground market
지하철	subway
직업	occupation, profession
직원	staff, employee
직장	workplace
직장인	office worker
직접	directly
진찰	examination, checkup
진찰하다	to examine, get a checkup
질문	question
질병	illness, disease
짐	luggage, load
집	home, house
집들이	housewarming
집안	household, family
집어넣다	to put something in
짜다	to be salty
짜리	worth
짧다	to be short
째	ordinal numbers

쪽	1. page; 2. side, direction
죽	straight
쯤	about, around
찍다	to take (a photo)
찜질방	Korean dry sauna
차	1. car; 2. tea
차고	garage
차다	1. to be cold; 2. to be full
차도	street, road
차례	ancestral rites
차리다	to set, fix (food)
차분하다	be calm, relaxed
차비	fare (bus, taxi)
차이	difference
차차	gradually
착하다	to be good-natured, kindhearted
참	1. really, truly; 2. by the way
참기름	sesame oil
찻길	street, road
창가 좌석	window seat
찾다	1. to find, look for; 2. to withdraw (money)
채널	channel
책	book
책방	bookstore
책상	desk
책장	bookshelf, bookcase
처럼	like, as
처방	prescription
처방하다	to prescribe
처음	the first time
천	textile
천천히	slow(ly)
첫	first
첫눈	first sight
청바지	blue jeans
청소	cleaning
청소기	vacuum cleaner
청소하다	to clean
초	1. candle; 2. beginning
초대	invitation
초대하다	to invite
초대장	invitation card
초등교육	elementary education
초등학교	elementary school
초등학생	elementary school student
초록색	green
초인종	doorbell
초콜릿	chocolate
촛불	candlelight
최고	the highest
최저	the lowest
추석	Korean Thanksgiving
추수	harvest
추워지다	to get colder
추천	recommendation
추천하다	to recommend
축구	soccer
축구하다	to play soccer
축하하다	to congratulate
출구	exit
출근	going to work
출근하다	to go to work
출발	departure
출발하다	to depart
춤	dance
춤(을) 추다	to dance
춥다	to be cold
취급	treatment
취미	hobby
취직	getting a job
취직하다	to get a job
층	floor, layer (counter)
치	amount for . . .
치다	1. to play (tennis); 2. to play (piano, guitar)
치료	treatment
치료하다	to treat, cure
치마	skirt
치약	toothpaste
치열하다	be intense, fierce
친구	friend
친절하다	to be kind, considerate
친척	relatives
친하다	be close to someone
칠판	blackboard
침	needle
침술	acupuncture
침대	bed
침실	bedroom
칫솔	toothbrush
카드	card
카메라	camera

캐나다	Canada
캠퍼스	campus
커다랗다	be large, huge
커피	coffee
커피숍	coffee shop, café
컴퓨터	computer
컴퓨터 랩	computer lab
케이블카	cable car
케이크	cake
켜다	to play (violin)
켤레	pair (counter)
코미디	comedy
코트	coat
콘서트	concert
콘택트 렌즈	contact lens
콜라	cola
콩나물	bean sprout
쿠바	Cuba
크게	loud(ly)
크다	to be big
크리스마스	Christmas
큰술	tablespoon
큰아버지	uncle (father's older brother)
큰일	matter of concern
클래스	class
클래식	classical music
클럽	club
키	height
키가 작다	to be short
키가 크다	to be tall
타고 가다	to go riding
타고 다니다	to come/go riding
타고 오다	to come riding
타다	1. to get in/on, ride; 2. to burn; 3. to win (a prize)
타이레놀	Tylenol
태권도	Taekwondo
태어나다	to be born
태우다	to give someone a ride
택배	delivery service
택시	taxi
택시비	taxi fare
테니스	tennis
테니스장	tennis court
테이프	tape
텔레비전	television
토마토	tomato
토요일	Saturday
토정비결	*Tojung* Secret (book)
통과하다	to pass through
통화	phone call
통화하다	to make a phone call
퇴근	leaving work
퇴근하다	to leave work
퇴원	discharge from a hospital
퇴원하다	to get discharged from a hospital
트럭	truck
특별하다	to be special
특히	particularly
틀다	to turn on, switch on, play (music)
티비	TV
티셔츠	T-shirt
티켓	ticket
팀	team
팁	tip
파	scallion
파란색	blue
파랗다	to be blue
파마	perm
파티	party
팔	arm
팔다	to sell
팔리다	to be sold
팬	pan
펜	pen
펴다	to open, unfold
편도	one-way trip
편리하다	to be convenient
편안하다	to be comfortable
편의점	convenience store
편지	letter
편하다	to be comfortable, convenient
포근하다	to be warm
포장	packing
폭포	waterfall
표	ticket
표정	(facial) expression
표지판	sign
푹	deeply, completely
풀다	to relieve
풀리다	to be relieved
풋볼	football
프랑스	France
프로(그램)	program
피곤하다	to be tired

피다 to bloom
피시방 Internet café
피아노 piano
피우다 to smoke
피자 pizza
피하다 to avoid
필기 (시험) written (exam)
필요하다 to be necessary
하고 1. and (with nouns); 2. with
하나 one
하나도 (not) at all
하늘 sky
하늘색 sky blue
하다 to do
하루 (one) day
하루 종일 all day
하마터면 almost
하숙방 a room in a boardinghouse
하숙비 boarding expenses
하숙집 boardinghouse
하얗다 to be white
하와이 Hawai'i
학교 school
학기 academic term
학년 school year
학벌 academic clique
학비 tuition fees
학생 student
학생회관 student center
학원 cram school
학점 (school) credit
한 one (with counter)
한국 Korea
한국말 the Korean language
한국어 the Korean language
한국학 Korean studies
한글 Korean alphabet
한글날 Hangeul Day
한라산 Halla Mount
한복 Korean traditional dress
한산하다 be quiet
한식 Korean food
한약 herbal tonic
한의학 Oriental medicine
한인타운 Koreatown
한자 Chinese character
한자어 Sino-Korean word
한테 to (a person or an animal)
한테서 from (a person or an animal)
할머니 grandmother
할아버지 grandfather
할인 discount
함께 together, along with
합격 pass, acceptance
합격하다 to pass, get accepted
항공료 airfare
항상 always
핸드폰 cellular phone
햄버거 hamburger
행 destined for
행복하다 to be happy
행사 event, function
허리 waist, back
허벅지 thigh
헤드폰 headphones
헤어지다 to break up
현관 (front) entrance
현금 cash
현명하다 be wise
현재 the present
형 the older brother of a male
형님*hon.* the older brother of a male
형제 sibling(s)
호 number, issue
호박 pumpkin, squash
호선 subway line
호주 Australia
호텔 hotel
혹시 by any chance
혼나다 to have a hard time
혼자 alone
홈런볼 home run ball
홍콩 Hong Kong
화랑 gallery
화려하다 to be fancy, colorful
화면 screen
화씨 Fahrenheit
화요일 Tuesday
화장 makeup
화장실 bathroom, restroom
화장품 cosmetics
화장하다 to apply makeup
환승 transfer
환승하다 to transfer (a ride)
활발하다 be animated

황소	bull, ox
회사	company
회식	get-together (work)
회의	meeting
횡단보도	crosswalk
후	after
후추	black pepper
후회	regret
후회하다	to regret
휴게실	lounge
휴식	rest
휴식하다	to take a rest
휴일	holiday, day off
휴지	toilet paper
흐려지다	to get cloudy
흐리다	to be cloudy
흔히	commonly
흰색	white
힘(이) 들다	to be hard

English-Korean Glossary

0 (zero)	영
0 (zero)	공 (phone #)
1	일
2	이
3	삼
4	사
a few days	며칠
a little	조금
	좀
a little later	이따가
a moment ago	방금
a pair of (counter)	벌
a while ago	아까
A.D.	서기
a.m.	오전
ability	실력
abnormality	이상
about	에 대해서
about, around	쯤
academic clique	학벌
academic term	학기
acceptance	합격
accessories	액세서리
accident	사고
according to	에 따라
account	계좌
action	액션
actor	배우
acupuncture	침술
adapt [to]	적응하다
adaptation	적응
address	주소
adjust [to]	맞추다
admission	입학(하다)
adult	어른
adult, (one's) elders	어른
affection	정
after	후
after a long time	오래간만
after a meal	식후
afternoon	오후
again	또
again	다시
age	나이*plain*
	연세*hon.*
age [to]	먹다 (나이를)
	나이가 들다
age group	연령대
air	공기
air-conditioner	에어컨
airfare	항공료
airplane	비행기
airport	공항
aisle	복도
Alaska	알래스카
alcoholic beverage	술
Alien Registration	외국인등록
all	다
	모두
all day	하루
	종일
all night long	밤새
all the time	언제나
all together	전부
almost	거의
	하마터면
alone	혼자
already	벌써
also, too	도
alter [to]	변하다
alteration	수선
alumni	동창회
always	항상
amount for . . .	치
amusement park	놀이공원
ancestor	조상
ancestral rites	차례
and	그리고
and (joins nouns)	와/과
	하고

and, also, too	또
animal (counter)	마리
answer	답
	대답
answer [to]	대답하다
answering machine	자동 응답기
antique	골동품
any	아무
anything	아무거나
anything particular	별일
apartment	아파트
apiece	씩
appetite	식성
apple	사과
apply [to]	바르다
apply [to]	지원하다
appoint [to]	지정하다
appreciation	감상(하다)
approximate	정도
approximately	약
aptitude	적성
architecture	건축학
area	분야
area code	지역 번호
arm	팔
arrange [to]	정리하다
arrive [to]	도착하다
art	예술
articles, goods	물품
as . . . as	만큼
as . . . as possible	되도록
Asia	아시아
Asian studies	동양학
ask [to]	묻다
ask a favor [to]	부탁하다
assignment	과제
at all [not]	하나도
at least	적어도
at, in, on (time)	에
athlete	선수
attend [to]	다니다
Australia	호주
automatically	저절로
automobile	자동차
autumn, fall	가을
avoid [to]	피하다
award	상
B.C.	기원전
baby	아기
back hair	뒷머리
back, behind	뒤
bag	가방
bakery	제과점
ballpoint pen	볼펜
bangs	앞머리
bank	은행
barber	이발사
barbershop	이발소
barely	겨우
bargain sale	바겐 세일
baseball	야구
	야구공
baseball stadium	야구장
basketball	농구
basketball game	농구 시합
bath	목욕
bathe [to]	목욕하다
bathroom	화장실
battery	배터리
be (equation) [to]	이다
be (existence) [to]	있다
be (existence), stay [to]	계시다*hon.*
be accepted [to]	붙다
be accurate [to]	정확하다
be adequate [to]	적당하다
be adequate [to]	적절하다
be aired [to]	방송되다
be all right, okay [to]	괜찮다
be amazing [to]	신기하다
be animated [to]	활발하다
be bad [to]	나쁘다
be beautiful [to]	아름답다
be big [to]	크다
be bitten [to]	물리다
be bitter [to]	쓰다
be black [to]	까맣다

be bland [to]	싱겁다
be blocked [to]	막히다
be blue [to]	파랗다
be bored [to]	심심하다
be boring [to]	지겹다
be born [to]	태어나다
be bright [to]	밝다
be busy [to]	바쁘다
be called [to]	불리다
be calm [to]	차분하다
be careful [to]	조심하다
be caught [to]	잡히다
be ceased [to]	중단되다
be changed [to]	바뀌다
be cheap [to]	싸다
be clean [to]	깨끗하다
be clear [to]	맑다
be close (to) [to]	친하다
be close to someone [to]	친하다
be close, near [to]	가깝다
be closed [to]	닫히다
be cloudy [to]	흐리다
be cold [to]	차다
	춥다
be comfortable [to]	편안하다
	편하다
be convenient [to]	편리하다
be cool, refreshing [to]	시원하다
be correct [to]	맞다
be crowded [to]	붐비다
be crowded [to]	복잡하다
be curious [to]	궁금하다
be dangerous [to]	위험하다
be dark [to]	어둡다
be deep [to]	깊다
be delicious [to]	맛있다
be deprived of [to]	뺏기다
be different [to]	다르다
be difficult [to]	어렵다
be dirty [to]	더럽다
be diverse [to]	다양하다
be dry [to]	건조하다
be early [to]	이르다
be easy [to]	쉽다
be envious of [to]	부럽다
be excited [to]	신나다
be excused [to]	실례하다
be expensive [to]	비싸다
be familiar [to]	익숙하다
be famous [to]	유명하다
be fancy, colorful [to]	화려하다
be far [to]	멀다
be fast [to]	빠르다
be fat [to]	뚱뚱하다
be few, scarce [to]	적다
be fierce [to]	치열하다
be flustered [to]	당황하다
be foggy [to]	(안개) 끼다
be formed [to]	생기다
be fortunate [to]	다행이다
be full [to]	차다
be glad [to]	반갑다
be good-natured [to]	착하다
be good, nice [to]	좋다
be handsome [to]	잘생기다
be happy [to]	행복하다
be hard [to]	힘(이) 들다
be healthy [to]	건강하다
be heavy [to]	무겁다
be high [to]	높다
be hot [to]	덥다
	뜨겁다
be hot and humid [to]	무덥다
be how [to]	어떻다
be huge [to]	커다랗다
be hungry [to]	배(가) 고프다
be identical [to]	똑같다
be important [to]	중요하다
be in fashion [to]	유행하다
be in school [to]	재학 중이다
be insufficient [to]	부족하다
be interesting, fun [to]	재미있다
be joyful [to]	즐겁다
be joyful, glad [to]	기쁘다
be kind [to]	친절하다
be late [to]	늦다

be light [to] 가볍다
be lonely [to] 외롭다
be long [to] 길다
be low [to] 낮다
be many, much [to] 많다
be mindless [to] 정신없다
be narrow [to] 좁다
be natural [to] 자연스럽다
be neat [to] 단정하다
be necessary [to] 필요하다
be new [to] 새롭다
be noisy [to] 시끄럽다
be open [to] 열리다
be over, finished [to] 끝나다
be passive [to] 소극적이다
be piled up [to] 쌓이다
be positive [to] 긍정적이다
be possible [to] 가능하다
be pretty [to] 예쁘다
be quiet [to] 한산하다
be quiet [to] 조용하다
be rare [to] 드물다
be red [to] 빨갛다
be refreshing [to] 상쾌하다
be regular [to] 규칙적(이다)
be related [to] 관련되다
be relieved [to] 풀리다
be reminded [to] 생각나다
be sad [to] 슬프다
아쉽다
be safe [to] 안전하다
be salty [to] 짜다
be scary, scared [to] 무섭다
be seen, visible [to] 보이다
be sensitive [to] 민감하다
be severe [to] 심하다
be short [to] 짧다
be short in height [to] 키가 작다
be sick [to] 아프다
be similar [to] 비슷하다
be skinny [to] 마르다
be sleepy [to] 졸리다
be slim [to] 날씬하다
be slippery [to] 미끄럽다
be small (in size) [to] 작다
조그맣다
be so [to] 그렇다
be sold [to] 팔리다
be sorry [to] 미안하다
죄송하다
be sour [to] 시다
be spacious, wide [to] 넓다
be special [to] 특별하다
be spicy [to] 맵다
be startled [to] 놀라다
be strange [to] 이상하다
be strong [to] 강하다
be stylish, attractive [to] 멋있다
be surprised [to] 놀라다
be sweet [to] 달다
be tall in height [to] 키가 크다
be tasteless [to] 맛없다
be thankful [to] 감사하다
고맙다
be thick [to] 굵다
be thick [to] 두껍다
be thin [to] 얇다
be thirsty [to] 목(이) 마르다
be tired [to] 피곤하다
be to one's liking [to] 마음에 들다
be troublesome [to] 귀찮다
be ugly [to] 못생기다
be uncomfortable [to] 불편하다
be undesirable [to] 싫다
be uninteresting [to] 재미없다
be unskilled [to] 서투르다
be urgent [to] 급하다
be used [to] 쓰이다
be warm [to] 따뜻하다
포근하다
be well [to] 안녕하다
be white [to] 하얗다
be wise [to] 현명하다
be wished [to] 기다려지다
be yellow [to] 노랗다
be young [to] 젊다

be young [to]	어리다
beach	바닷가
bean sprout	콩나물
beautiful woman	미인
beauty salon	미용실
because	왜냐하면
because of	때문에
become [to]	되다
become cooler [to]	시원해지다
bed	침대
bedroom	침실
beef	소고기
before	전
beg [to]	빌다
begin [to]	시작하다
beginning	초
below the freezing point	영하
between	사이
between, among	중에서
beverage	음료수
bicycle	자전거
biology	생물학
birthday	생일*plain*
	생신*hon.*
bite [to]	물다
black	검정색
black (=까망)	까만색
black pepper	후추
blackboard	칠판
blessing	복
bloom [to]	피다
blouse	블라우스
blow [to]	불다
blue	파란색
blue jeans	청바지
boarding expenses	하숙비
boardinghouse	하숙집
boast [to]	자랑하다
body	몸
body character	신체특성
body parts	신체부위
boil [to]	끓다
	끓이다
book	책
bookshelf	책장
bookstore	책방
	서점
boots	장화
borrow [to]	빌리다
Boston	보스톤
both parties	양측
bottom [the], below	밑
bowl	그릇
bowling	볼링
box	박스
	상자
bread	빵
break [to]	깨다
break [to]	깨지다
break down [to]	고장나다
break up [to]	헤어지다
breakdown	고장
breakfast	아침
bride	신부
briefly	잠시
bring [to]	갖고 오다
bring and put down somewhere [to]	갖다 놓다
bring/take something to someone [to]	갖다
	드리다*hon.*
bring/take something to someone [to]	갖다 주다*plain*
broadcasting station	방송국
Broadway theater	브로드웨이 극장
broth	국물
brush one's teeth [to]	이(를) 닦다
bubble	거품
Buddhism	불교
Buddhist temple	절
building	건물
	빌딩
building, structure	건축물
Bulguksa	불국사
bull, ox	황소
bundle, bunch (counter)	단

bus	버스
business	사업
business	영업
but, however	그런데
	그렇지만
butcher shop	정육점
buy [to]	사다
buy and eat [to]	사 먹다
buy one's groceries [to]	장(을) 보다
by any chance	혹시
by chance, accident	우연히
by means of	으로
by the way	그런데, 근데
	참
cable car	케이블카
cake	케이크
calendar	달력
call [to]	걸다
call out [to]	부르다
camera	카메라
campus	캠퍼스
Canada	캐나다
candle	초
candlelight	촛불
cannot	못
cap, hat	모자
capital city	수도
car	차
card	카드
care for [to]	위하다
care of health	몸조리
carrot	당근
carry around [to]	갖고 다니다
case	경우
cash	현금
catch [to]	잡다
catch, grab [to]	잡다
cellular phone	핸드폰
Celsius	섭씨
cent	센트
center [the], pivot	중심지
central districts [the]	중부 지방
Central Post Office [the]	중앙 우체국

century	세기
chair	의자
champagne	샴페인
change [to]	변화하다
change (clothes) [to]	갈아 입다
change (money)	거스름돈
change (vehicles) [to]	갈아 타다
change, switch [to]	바꾸다
channel	채널
check, bill	계산서
Chicago	시카고
child	아이
	어린이
children	아이들
	자녀
China	중국
Chinese character	한자
Chinese food	중식
chocolate	초콜릿
choice	선택
choose, select [to]	고르다
	선택하다
chopsticks	젓가락
Christmas	크리스마스
church	교회
cigarette	담배
city	도시
city hall	시청
city hall station	시청역
civilization	문명
class	반
	클래스
classical music	클래식
classroom	교실
clean [to]	청소하다
cleaner's	세탁소
cleaning	청소
clerk, salesperson	점원
clock, watch	시계
close [to]	닫다
close, cover [to]	덮다
closet	옷장
clothes	옷

clothing habits	의생활	connect, link [to]	연결하다
clothing store	옷가게	connection	인연 (people)
cloud	구름	connection, link	연결
club	클럽	consist of	이루어지다
club (amateur)	동호회	consistently	지속적으로
coat	코트	construction	공사
coffee	커피	contact	연락
coffee shop, café	커피숍	contact [to]	연락하다
cola	콜라	contact lens	콘택트 렌즈
collapse [to]	쓰러지다	contain [to]	들어있다
collect [to]	모으다	continue [to]	계속되다
college entrance exam	입시		계속하다
college student	대학생	continuously	계속
college, university	대학	convenience store	편의점
	대학교	cook [to]	요리하다
color	색, 색깔	cooked rice	밥
come [to]	오다	cooking	요리
come around [to]	놀러오다	cosmetics	화장품
come in [to]	들어오다	cost money [to]	돈이 들다
come on foot [to]	걸어오다	cost of living	물가
come out [to]	나오다	cough	기침
come out to greet someone [to]	마중 나오다	cough [to]	기침하다
		counseling	상담
come riding [to]	타고 오다	country	나라
come to think of it	그러고 보니	course, class	수업
come/go riding [to]	타고 다니다	course, subject	과목
comedy	코미디	cracker	과자
comic book	만화책	craftwork	공예품
comic book rental store	만화방	cram school	학원
commencement	졸업식	credit card	신용 카드
commonly	흔히	cross [to]	건너다
communication	소통	crossroads, intersection	사거리
company	회사	cry [to]	울다
competition	경쟁(하다)	Cuba	쿠바
complement [to]	보충하다	culture	문화
completely	완전히	current affairs	시사
computer	컴퓨터	cut (hair) [to]	자르다 (for men)
computer lab	컴퓨터 랩	cut (something for someone) [to]	잘라 주다*plain*
concert	음악회		잘라 드리다*hum.*
	콘서트	cut down [to]	깎다
condiment, seasoning	양념	Dabo Tower	다보탑
condition	조건	daily life, living	생활
congratulate [to]	축하하다		

dance	춤
dance [to]	춤(을) 추다
Dano day	단오
date	날짜
	데이트
date [to]	데이트하다
	사귀다
date of birth	생년월일
dating	연애(하다)
daughter	딸*plain*
	따님*hon.*
dawn	새벽
day	날
day (counter)	일
day [one]	하루
day after tomorrow [the]	모레
daytime	낮
decide [to]	정하다
decrease [to]	줄이다
deeply	푹
deer antler	녹용
degree	도
deliver [to]	배달하다
delivery	배달
delivery service	택배
depart [to]	출발하다
department store	백화점
departure	출발
desk	책상
dessert	디저트
destined for	행
detergent	세제
develop [to]	발달시키다
	발달하다
development	발달
dialect	사투리
dictionary	사전
die [to]	죽다
diet	다이어트
difference	차이
digestion	소화
digit	자리
diligently	열심히
dining table	식탁
dinner	저녁
directly	바로
	직접
disappear [to]	없어지다
discharge (hospital)	퇴원(하다)
discount	할인
discount stores	할인 마트
disease	병
disease	질병
dish	그릇
dishwashing	설거지(하다)
dislike [to]	싫어하다
distance	거리
do [to]	하다
do homework [to]	숙제하다
do not	안
do the laundry [to]	빨래하다
do wrong [to]	잘못하다
doctor	의사
dog	개
dollar	달러
	불
domestic flight	국내선
Dongdaemun Market	동대문시장
door	문
doorbell	초인종
dormitory	기숙사
downstairs	아래층
downtown	시내
doze off [to]	졸다
drama	드라마
draw [to]	그리다
drawer	서랍
dream a dream [to]	꿈(을) 꾸다
dress [one-piece]	원피스
dress shirt	와이셔츠
dress shoes	구두
dress someone [to]	입히다
drink [to]	마시다
drive [to]	운전하다
driver	기사
driver's license	운전 면허

driving	운전
drop out of [to]	빠지다
drugstore	약국
drum	드럼
dry [to]	말리다
during	동안
e-mail	이메일
each	각
each other	서로
early	일찍
earn (money) [to]	벌다
earn money [to]	돈을 벌다
earring	귀걸이
east	동
East Coast	동부
East Hall	이스트 홀
eat [to]	드시다*hon.*
	먹다*plain*
eat out [to]	외식하다
economics	경제학
economy-class seat	일반석
education	교육학
egg	계란
electrical engineering	전기공학
elementary education	초등교육
elementary school	초등학교
elementary school student	초등학생
elevator	엘리베이터
employee	종업원
end [to]	끝내다
engagement	약혼
English language [the]	영어
enjoy [to]	즐기다
enter [to]	들어가다
entertainment	예능
entrance	입구
entrance [front]	현관
envelope	봉투
et cetera	등
Europe	유럽
evening	저녁
event	행사
event	일
every day	날마다
	매일
every month	매달
every week	매주
every year	매년
everywhere	곳곳
examination, checkup	진찰
examine, checkup [to]	진찰하다
exceed [to]	넘다
exercise	연습 문제
	운동
exercise [to]	운동하다
exit	출구
experience	경험
experience [to]	경험하다
eyeglasses	안경
eyes	눈
face	얼굴
facial expression	표정
fact, truth	사실
factory	공장
Fahrenheit	화씨
fall (down) [to]	넘어지다
fall asleep [to]	잠(이) 들다
fall foliage	단풍
fall in love [to]	반하다
family	가족
family member	식구
fare (bus, taxi)	차비
farming	농사
fashion, trend	유행
fast, quickly	빨리
father	아버지
feast, party	잔치
fee, fare	요금
feed [to]	먹이다
feeling	기분
feeling, sense	느낌
fever	열
fifteen days	보름
fight [to]	싸우다
find, look for [to]	찾다

find out, check out [to]	알아보다
finish [to]	마치다
fire	불
fire station	소방서
first	첫
first, beforehand	먼저
first, most	제일
first birthday [the]	돌
first sight	첫눈
first son	장남
first-class seat	일등석
first-time [the]	처음
fish	생선
fishery	어업
fit [to]	맞다
five days	닷새
fix (food) [to]	차리다
fix up [to]	손질하다
flesh, fat	살
floor	바닥
floor, layer (counter)	층
floor heating system	온돌
flower	꽃
flower shop	꽃집
flu	독감
fog	안개
Folk Village	민속촌
food	음식
food cost	음식값
food expenses	식비
foot	발
football	풋볼
for, in order to	위한
for, per	에
for a long time	오랫동안
for a short time	잠깐만
for example	예를 들어
foreign country	외국
foreign language	외국어
foreigner	외국인
forget [to]	잊어버리다
forget [to]	잊다
fortunately	다행히
fortune	운세
fortune-teller	점술인
four days	나흘
fracture [to]	부러지다
France	프랑스
free	공짜
free of charge	무료
free time	여가
freeze [to]	얼다
freshman	1학년
Friday	금요일
friend	친구
from (a person or an animal)	한테서
from (location)	에서
from (time)	에서
from (time) . . .	부터
from next time	다음부터(는)
front [the]	앞
fruit	과일
function, work [to]	되다
furniture	가구
furniture store	가구점
gain [to]	얻다
gain weight [to]	살이 찌다
gallery	화랑
game	게임
game, match	시합
Gangwon region	강원
garage	차고
garlic	마늘
gas station	주유소
gate	대문
gather [to]	모이다
gathering	모임
generally, mostly	대체로
get, turn into [to]	되다
get a job	취직(하다)
get a job [to]	(직장에) 들어가다
get along [to]	지내다
get around [to]	다니다
get busier [to]	바빠지다

get cloudy [to]	구름이 끼다 흐려지다
get colder [to]	추워지다
get in/on, ride [to]	타다
get lower [to]	낮아지다
get married [to]	결혼하다
get off [to]	내리다
get out of	벗어나다
get someone to sleep [to]	재우다
get up [to]	일어나다
get-together (work)	회식
gift certificate	상품권
ginseng	인삼
girlfriend	여자 친구
give [to]	드리다*hum.* 주다*plain*
give a present, gift [to]	선물하다
give someone a ride [to]	태우다
glass, cup	잔
gloves	장갑
go [to]	가다
go and get back [to]	다녀 오다
go down (the Sun) [to]	지다
go down [to]	내려가다
go on an outing [to]	놀러가다
go on foot [to]	걸어가다
go out [to]	나가다
go out to greet someone [to]	마중 나가다
go riding [to]	타고 가다
go up [to]	올라가다
going to work	출근(하다)
gold ring	금반지
golf	골프
good fortune	복
gourmet	별미
government official	정부 관료
grade	성적
gradually	점점
gradually	차차
graduate [to]	졸업하다
graduate school	대학원
graduate student	대학원생
graduation	졸업
gram	그램
grandfather	할아버지
grandmother	할머니
green	초록색
green tea	녹차
greet [to]	인사하다
greeting	인사
groom	신랑
grow up [to]	자라다
guard, protect [to]	지키다
guest, customer	손님
guitar	기타
gwageo exam	과거 시험
Gwanak Mountain	관악산
Gyeongju	경주
hair	머리
hair dryer	드라이어
haircut (for men)	이발(하다)
hairstylist	미용사
half	반
half moon	반달
half price	반값
Halla Mount	한라산
hamburger	햄버거
hand	손
Hangeul Day	한글날
happen, break out	[noun] 나다
hardship	고생
harvest	추수
have (a ceremony) [to]	지내다
have [to]	있다
have, catch a cold [to]	감기에 걸리다
have a difficult time [to]	고생하다
have a full stomach [to]	배(가) 부르다
have a hard time [to]	혼나다
have a meal [to]	식사하다
have one's parents with [to]	(부모를) 모시다
have something ahead [to]	앞두다
Hawai'i	하와이
head	머리

headphones	헤드폰	how	어떻게
heart, mind	마음씨	how long/much	얼마
heat [to]	달구다	how long/much	얼마나
heating	난방	how many, what	몇
heel	굽	human being	인간
height	키	hurry [to]	서두르다
hello (on the phone)	여보세요	hurt [to]	다치다
help	도움	husband	남편
help [to]	돕다	I	나*plain*
	도와 주다*plain*		저*hum.*
	도와드리다*hum.*	I see	네
herbal tonic	한약	ice	얼음
here	여기	ice cream	아이스크림
high school	고등학교	ice hockey	아이스하키
high school senior	고3	identification card	신분증
high school student	고등학생	if possible	웬만하면
high-rise building	고층빌딩	ignore [to]	무시하다
higher education	고등교육	improve [to]	늘다
highest [the]	최고	in, at (dynamic location)	에서
highway, freeway	고속도로	in, at, on (static location)	에
hike [to]	등산하다	in advance	미리
hiking	등산	in peace	안녕히
history	역사	in the future	앞으로
hobby	취미	Incheon	인천
holiday, day off	휴일	including	까지
home, house	집*plain*	increase [to]	늘다
	댁*hon.*	increase [to]	증진시키다
home run ball	홈런볼	inform [to]	알리다
hometown	고향	informal speech	반말
homework	숙제	information	정보
honey, dear	여보	ingredient	재료
honeymoon	신혼여행	inquire [to]	물어보다
Hong Kong	홍콩	Insadong	인사동
honorific noun suffix	님	insect	벌레
horror movie	공포 영화	inside [the]	안
hospital	병원	instant noodles (ramen)	라면
hospitalization	입원(하다)	instead of	대신
hot shredded-beef soup	육개장	interest	관심
hotel	호텔	international call	국제 전화
hour, o'clock	시	international flight	국제선
household, family	집안	Internet	인터넷
housekeeping, living	살림	Internet café	피시방
housewarming	집들이	intersection, crossroads	네거리

interview	면접
interview	인터뷰
interview site	면접장
interviewer	면접관
introduce [to]	소개하다
introduce someone [to]	소개하다
introduction	소개
invitation	초대
invite [to]	초대하다
invitation card	초대장
island	섬
Italy	이태리
item (counter)	개
jacket	자켓
Jamsil	잠실
Japan	일본
Japanese food	일식
japchae	잡채
jazz	재즈
Jeju Island	제주도
joke	농담
Joseon dynasty	조선시대
journal	일기
juice	주스
jumper/jacket	점퍼
junior	3학년
junior college	전문대학
just, just in time	마침
just, without any special reason	그냥
kalbi (spareribs)	갈비
karaoke room	노래방
key	열쇠
kimbap	김밥
kimchi	김치
kitchen	부엌
knock [to]	두드리다
know [to]	알다
Korea	한국
Korean airline	대한항공
Korean alphabet	한글
Korean dry sauna	찜질방
Korean food	한식
Korean language	한국말
	한국어
Korean studies	한국학
Korean Thanksgiving	추석
Korean wrestling	씨름
Koreatown	한인타운
lab	랩
lack [to]	부족하다
lack [to]	모자라다
lamp	램프
last	마지막
last, past	지난
last night	어젯밤
last year	작년
late	늦게
lateness	지각(하다)
later	나중에
laugh [to]	웃다
law	법학
law school	법대
learn [to]	배우다
leave (a message) [to]	남기다
leave [to]	떠나다
leaving work	퇴근(하다)
left side	왼쪽
leg	다리
lend [to]	빌려주다
less	덜
lesson, chapter	과
letter	편지
lettuce	상추
library	도서관
licorice	감초
lie down [to]	눕다
life	인생
light	불
like [to]	좋아하다
like, as	처럼
	같이
like, as if	마치
like this	이렇게
linguistics	언어학
listen [to]	듣다

literature	문학
live [to]	살다
live on one's own [to]	자취하다
living on one's own	자취
living room	거실
location	위치
London	런던
long life	장수
long time	오래
long weekend	연휴
long-distance call	장거리 전화
look around,	구경하다
Los Angeles (L.A.)	로스 앤젤레스
lose [to]	잃어버리다
lose, be defeated [to]	지다
loud(ly)	크게
lounge	휴게실
	라운지
love	사랑
love [to]	사랑하다
lowest [the]	최저
luck, fortune	운
luggage, load	짐
lunar calendar	음력
lunch	점심
magazine	잡지
mail (a letter, parcel) [to]	부치다
mail service	우편
main character	주인공
major	전공
major [to]	전공하다
make [to]	만들다
make a phone call [to]	통화하다
	전화하다
make friends [to]	사귀다
make noise [to]	떠들다
make someone cry [to]	울리다
make someone laugh [to]	웃기다
make time [to]	내다 (시간을)
makeup	화장(하다)
man	남자
man, male	남성
manicure	손톱 손질
many, several	여러
map	지도
market	마켓
marketplace	시장
marriage	결혼
married couple	부부
mart	마트
massage	마사지
master bedroom	안방
match, game	경기
match, suit [to]	어울리다
matchmaking	중매
material	재료
matter of concern	큰일
meal	밥
	식사
mean, signify [to]	뜻하다
meaning	뜻
meaning	의미
meantime	그동안
meat	고기
mechanical engineering	기계 공학
medical school	의대
medical technology	의학기술
medicinal ingredients	약재
medicine	약
meet [to]	만나다
meeting	회의
memorable	인상적
memorize [to]	외우다
memory	기억
men and women	남녀
menu	메뉴
merchandise, stuff	물건
message	메시지
meter	미터기
method	방법
Mexico	멕시코
middle [the]	중간
middle, center [the]	가운데
middle school	중학교
middle school student	중학생
middle-aged woman	아주머니

milk	우유	name	성함*hon.*
million	백만		이름*plain*
mind, heart	마음	nap	낮잠
minor	부전공	national	국가적
minute (counter)	분	national holidays	국경일
miss [to]	놓치다	nature	자연
miss, long for [to]	그립다	navy blue, indigo	남색
mistake	실수(하다)	nearby, vicinity	근처
mister	아저씨	necklace	목걸이
mom	엄마	necktie	넥타이
Monday	월요일	needle	침
money	돈	neighbor, neighborhood	이웃
month (counter)	개월	neighborhood	동네
	월	never	절대
	달	new	새
moon	달	New Year	새해
more	더	New Year's bow	세배
more or less	다소	New Year's cash gift	세뱃돈
morning	아침	New Year's Day	설날
mosquito	모기	New York	뉴욕
most [the]	가장	newly	새로
mostly	대부분	newlywed couple	신혼 부부
mostly, mainly	주로	news	소식
motel	모텔		뉴스
mother	어머니	newspaper	신문
mountain climber	등산객	newspaper publisher	신문사
mousse	무스	next, following	다음
move [to]	이사하다	next year	내년
move, shift [to]	옮기다	night	밤
movie	영화	no	아니요
movie theater	극장	no matter how	아무리
much, many	많이	noodles	면
muffler	목도리	north	북
mugwort	쑥	not at all	전혀
museum	박물관	not be (existence) [to]	없다
music	음악	not be (negative equation) [to]	아니다
musical instrument	악기	not even one	하나도
musical performance	연주	not have [to]	없다
my	제*hum.*	not know [to]	모르다
	내*plain*	not N1 but N2	말고
naengmyŏn (cold buckwheat noodles)	냉면	not really	별로
Nam Mountain	남산	not to be, not do [to]	않다

nothing but, only	밖에
novel	소설
now	지금
	이젠(이제+는)
number	번호
	숫자
number (counter)	번
number, issue	호
number of times	번
nurture (one's aptitude) [to]	(적성) 살리다
object particle	을/를
occupation, profession	직업
of	의
of course, naturally	당연히
office	사무실
office worker	직장인
often, frequently	자주
oh	아
	어
oh my	아이고
Oh! Oh my! Dear me!	어머
okay	네
old days	예전
old days [the]	옛날
older brother of a female [the]	오빠
older brother of a male [the]	형
older brother of a male [the]	형님*hon.*
older sister of a female [the]	언니
older sister of a male [the]	누나
Olympics	올림픽
on the other hand	반면(에)
once in a while	가끔씩
one	하나
one (with counter)	한
one and only	유일한
one part	일부분
one portion	일 인 분
oneself	본인
one-way trip	편도
one's specialty	전문
onion	양파
only	만
open [to]	열다
open, unfold [to]	펴다
opera	오페라
opinion	의견
opponent	상대편
opposite	반대
oral exam	구두 시험
order [to]	주문하다
order (food) [to]	시키다
order, turn	순서
ordinal numbers	번째 (counter) 째
Oriental medicine	한의학
other side [the]	건너편
outside	밖
outside [the]	야외
over there	저기
over time	시간이 흐르면서
overlap [to]	겹치다
oversleep	늦잠
oversleep [to]	늦잠자다
owner	주인
pack [to]	싸다
pack, bag	봉지
packing	포장
page	쪽
pair	켤레
pan	팬
pants	바지
paper	종이
parcel, package	소포
parents	부모님
park	공원
parking lot	주차장
part	부분
part-time job	아르바이트

particularly	유난히
	특히
party	파티
pass [to]	지나다 (시간)
pass away [to]	돌아가시다*hon.*
pass by [to]	지나가다
pass through	통과하다
passport	여권
pay (money) [to]	돈을 내다
pear	배
pedestrian crossing	횡단보도
pen	펜
pencil	연필
people (counter)	명*plain*
	분*hon.*
perform on a musical instrument [to]	연주하다
period	시대
period (of time)	기간
perm	파마
person, people	사람
personality	성격
pharmacist	약사
phone call	통화(하다)
photo, picture	사진
physics	물리학
piano	피아노
pibimbap	비빔밥
picture, painting	그림
pills (counter)	알
pizza	피자
place, location	곳
	데
	장소
place, spot	군데
plan	계획
plan [to]	계획하다
plate	접시
	그릇
play, drama	연극
play, not work [to]	놀다
play (piano, guitar) [to]	치다
play (tennis) [to]	치다
play (violin) [to]	켜다
play baseball [to]	야구하다
play basketball [to]	농구하다
play soccer [to]	축구하다
playground	운동장
pluck [to]	따다
plural particle	들
point, aspect	점
police	경찰
police station	경찰서
political science	정치학
popularity	인기
population	인구
post office	우체국
post up [to]	올리다
postage	우편 요금
postal code	우편 번호
postbox	우체통
postcard	엽서
postman	우체부
potato	감자
practice	연습
practice [to]	연습하다
preparation	준비
prepare [to]	준비하다
prescription	처방(하다)
present [the]	현재
present, gift	선물
president	대통령
presidential election	대통령 선거
price	가격
	값
prize; merchandise	상품
probably, perhaps	아마
problem	문제
process	과정
professor	교수님
professor's office	연구실
program	프로(그램)
promise	약속
pronunciation	발음
properly	제대로
prosperity	번영

protect [to]	지키다
psychology	심리학
pub, bar	술집
public [the]	대중
public bathhouse	목욕탕
pulgogi (roasted meat)	불고기
pumpkin, squash	호박
purchase [to]	장만하다
push [to]	누르다
put (footwear) on someone [to]	신기다
put emphasis on	중시하다
put forth effort [to]	수고하다
put in [to]	넣다
put on [to]	얹다
put something down for someone [to]	놓아 주다
put something in [to]	집어넣다
put something into something	담다
quantity	양
question	질문
quick(ly)	어서
radio	라디오
rain	비
rain [to]	비(가) 오다
rainy season	장마
raise [to]	길러내다
read [to]	독서하다
	읽다
reading	독서
really, truly	정말
	참
receipt	영수증
receive [to]	받다
recipe	만드는 법
recommend [to]	추천하다
recommendation	추천
record [to]	녹음하다
recording	녹음
recover [to]	낫다
red	빨간색
red-pepper paste	고추장
refrigerator	냉장고
regardless of	상관없이
regards	안부
region, district	지방
registered (mail)	등기
regret	후회
regret [to]	후회하다
regular	보통
regular price	정가
regulations	규칙
relation, connection	관련
relationship	관계
relationship	사이
relatively	비교적
relatives	친척
relieve [to]	풀다
remain [to]	남다
	남아있다
remember [to]	기억나다/하다
remember [to]	기억하다
repeat after [to]	따라하다
reply	답장
reply [to]	답장하다
reporter	기자
resemble [to]	닮다
reservation	예약(하다)
reserve [to]	예약하다
Resident Registration card	주민등록증
Resident Registration number	주민등록번호
rest	휴식
rest [to]	쉬다
restaurant	식당
	음식점
restroom	화장실
retake the exam	재수(하다)
return, come back [to]	돌아오다
return (something to someone) [to]	돌려 드리다*hum.*
return (something to someone) [to]	돌려 주다*plain*
return (to) [to]	돌아가다

review	복습	season	계절
rice cake	떡	season [to]	양념하다
rice cake soup	떡국	seat	자리
ride pass, ticket	승차권		좌석
right away, soon	곧	seat belt	안전 벨트
right side	오른쪽	seaweed soup	미역국
ring	반지	second	두 번째
rise, come up [to]	뜨다	secondary education	중등교육
road	찻길	see [to]	뵙다*hum.*
rock music	록	see, look, watch [to]	보다*plain*
rock-paper-scissors	가위바위보	selection	선택(하다)
role	역할	self	본인
roll	롤	self-identification	본인 확인
room	방	self-introduction	자기 소개
room in a boardinghouse	하숙방	sell [to]	팔다
roommate	룸메이트	send [to]	보내다
rough map	약도	senior	4학년
roughly	대충	Seokga Tower	석가탑
round trip	왕복	Seokguram (stone cave)	석굴암
rumor	소문	Seorak Mount	설악산
run [to]	뛰다	Seoul	서울
Russia	러시아	Seoul National University Station	서울대입구역
salary	월급	Seoul Tower	서울타워
sale	세일	separately	따로
sand	모래	serious matter	중대사
sandals	샌들	serve [to]	대접하다
sandwich	샌드위치	service	서비스
Saturday	토요일	sesame oil	참기름
sauna	사우나	set	세트
save [to]	살리다	sex, gender	성별
scallion	파	shampoo	샴푸
scarf	목도리	shape	모양
scenery, view	경치	share [to]	나누다
scholarship	장학금	shaving	면도(하다)
school	학교	shirt	셔츠
school credit	학점	shoes	신발
school uniform	교복	shop [to]	쇼핑하다
school vacation	방학	shopping	쇼핑
school year	학년	shopping district	상가
science	과학	shorten [to]	줄이다
screen	화면	shorts	반바지
sea	바다	show	쇼
search for [to]	구하다		

show, represent [to]	나타내다	snow [to]	눈(이) 오다
shower	샤워	so	그러니까
sibling(s)	형제	so, therefore	그래서
side, beside [the]	옆	so far yet	여태
side, direction	쪽	soap	비누
side dishes	반찬	soccer	축구
sidewalk	인도	social activities	사회 활동
sightseeing	구경	social club	동아리
sign	표지판	Social Security number	사회보장번호
sign, signature	사인	society	사회
signification	의미(하다)	socks, stockings	양말
Silla	신라	sofa	소파
sincerely yours	올림*hon.*	soft tofu stew	순두부찌개
sing (a song) [to]	부르다	solar calendar	양력
sing [to]	노래 부르다	some (time, amount)	얼마
	노래하다	some kind of	무슨
singer	가수	someone	누가
single out [to]	뽑다		누구
single room	독방	something	뭐
Sino-Korean word	한자어	sometime	언제
sit [to]	앉다	sometimes	가끔
situation	상황	somewhere	어디
size	사이즈	son	아들
ski	스키	song	노래
ski [to]	스키 타다	*songpyeon*	송편
skill	솜씨	soon	금방
skirt	치마	sophomore	2학년
sky	하늘	sound, noise	소리
sky blue	하늘색	soup	국
sleep	잠		스프
sleep [to]	자다*plain*	south	남
	주무시다*hon.*	South America	남미
	잠을 자다	Southeast Asia	동남아
sleeve	소매	Southern	남부
slice [to]	썰다	soy sauce	간장
slightly	살짝	soybean-paste stew	된장찌개
slightly	약간	spaghetti	스파게티
slipper	슬리퍼	Spain	스페인
slow(ly)	천천히	speak [to]	말하다
smell	냄새	speech, words	말씀*hon.*
smell [to]	냄새 나다		말*plain*
smoke [to]	피우다	spend time [to]	보내다
snow	눈	spicy rice cake	떡볶이

spinach	시금치
spoon	숟가락
spoons and chopsticks	수저
sports	스포츠
sports shoes, sneakers	운동화
sports stadium	경기장
spread out [to]	깔다
spring	봄
staff, employee	직원
stairs	계단
stamp	우표
stand [to]	서다
stand up [to]	일어서다
standard	기준
star	별
station	역
stay up all night [to]	(밤을) 새우다
stick, affix [to]	붙이다
still	여전히
stir-fry [to]	볶다
stomach	위
stomach, abdomen	배
stop [bus]	정류장
stop, pull over [to]	세우다
stop by [to]	들르다
store	가게
	상점
store signs	간판
straight	쭉
straight, upright	똑바로
street, road	거리
	차도
	찻길
	길
stress	스트레스
student	학생
student abroad	유학생
student center	학생회관
studio apartment	원룸
study	공부
study [to]	공부하다
study room	공부방
style	스타일
subject particle	께서*hon.*
	이/가*plain*
subway	지하철
subway line	호선
suddenly	갑자기
sugar	설탕
suit, formal dress	정장
summer	여름
summer/winter term	계절 학기
Sunday	일요일
supermarket	슈퍼(마켓)
surely	꼭
surely, certainly	반드시
sushi	스시
sweater	스웨터
swim [to]	수영하다
swimming	수영
swimming pool	수영장
Sydney	시드니
symbolize [to]	상징하다
symptom	증상
T-shirt	티셔츠
table	상
table legs	상다리
tablespoon	큰술
Taekwondo	태권도
take [to]	갖고 가다
take, carry [to]	가져가다
take (a photo) [to]	찍다
take [time] [to]	걸리다
take a course [to]	듣다
take a shower [to]	샤워하다
take off, undress [to]	벗다
take out [to]	꺼내다
take someone's clothes off [to]	벗기다
talk, chat	이야기
	얘기
talk, chat [to]	이야기하다
	얘기하다
tangerine	귤
tape	테이프
taste [to]	맛보다

taxi 택시
taxi fare 택시비
tea 차
teach [to] 가르치다
teacher 선생님
teacher's wife 사모님
team 팀
telephone 전화
telephone bill 전화비
telephone number 전화번호
television 텔레비전
tell, convey [to] 전하다
temperature 기온
temple 사찰
ten days 열흘
tennis 테니스
tennis court 테니스장
test, exam 시험
text message 문자
textbook 교과서
textile 천
than 보다
that 그
that (over there) 저
that is 즉
that kid 걔
the moment 순간
the side of the head 옆머리
the whole nation 전국
the winner 우승자
then, if so 그럼
then, in that case 그러면
there 거기
these days 요새
요즘
thesis 논문
thief 도둑
thigh 허벅지
thing 것
거
things to eat 먹거리
things to watch 볼거리
thinly 얇게
this 이
이거 (=이것)
this time 이번
this way 이쪽(으로)
this year 올해
thread 실
three days 사흘
thriller 스릴러
throat 목
Thursday 목요일
ticket 티켓
표
ticket office 매표소
tie [to] 매다
tightly 꽉
time 때
time, hour (duration) 시간
tip 팁
to (a person) 한테
께*hon.*
to (destination) 에
to be rejected [to] 떨어지다
to burn [to] 타다
to fall [to] 떨어지다
to get damaged [to] 상하다
to look like [to] 생기다
to spoil [to] 상하다
to win (a prize) [to] 타다
to/until/through (time) 까지
today 오늘
tofu 두부
together 함께
같이
together, along with 함께
toilet paper 휴지
Tojung Secret (book) 토정비결
Tokyo 도쿄
tomato 토마토
tomorrow 내일
too much 너무
tooth 이
toothbrush 칫솔
toothpaste 치약

top side [the], above 위
topic particle ('as for') 은/는
touch [to] 건드리다
toward, to 으로
town shuttle bus 마을 버스
tradition 전통
traditional culture 전통 문화
traditional holidays 명절
traditional Korean dress 한복
traditional teahouse 전통 찻집
traffic 교통
traffic light 신호등
traffic sign 교통 표지판
train 기차
train [to] 길러내다
transfer (a ride) [to] 환승(하다)
transportation card 교통카드
travel [to] 여행하다
travel agency 여행사
travel, trip 여행
treat [to] 대접하다
treatment 취급
treatment 치료(하다)
trim [to] 다듬다
truck 트럭
Tuesday 화요일
tuition fees 학비
turn (the channel) [to] 돌리다
turn [to] 돌다
turn in (homework) [to] 내다
turn off [to] 끄다
turn on (electronics) [to] 틀다
turn on, switch on, play (music) [to] 틀다
TV 티비
two 둘
two (with counter) 두
two days 이틀
Tylenol 타이레놀
uh (expression of hesitation) 저어
umbrella 우산
uncle 삼촌
uncle (father's older brother) 큰아버지
underground market 지하 상가
underpass 지하도
understand [to] 이해하다
understand, recognize [to] 알아듣다
uniform 유니폼
Union Building 유니온 빌딩
United Kingdom [the] 영국
United States [the] 미국
up to (location) 까지
use [to] 사용하다
쓰다
used furniture 중고 가구
used merchandise 중고품
usually 보통
utilize [to] 이용하다
vacuum cleaner 청소기
Vancouver 밴쿠버
vegetable 야채
vending machine 표 발매기
very much 굉장히
무척
very, really 아주
video, movie file 동영상
violin 바이올린
visa 비자
visit (someone sick) 문병(하다)
vocabulary 단어
voice 목소리
volume (counter) 권
waist, back 허리
wait [to] 기다리다
wake someone up [to] 깨우다
wake up [to] 깨다
walk [to] 걷다
walk around [to] 걸어다니다
wallet 지갑
want [to] 원하다
wardrobe, closet 옷장
wash (hair) [to] 감다
wash dishes [to] 설거지하다

wash one's face [to]	세수하다
wash one's hands [to]	손(을) 씻다
wash someone's hair [to]	감기다
washing machine	세탁기
water	물
waterfall	폭포
way	길
we/us/our	우리*plain*
	저희*hum.*
wealthy person	부자
wear, put on (clothes) [to]	입다
wear (footwear) [to]	신다
wear (glasses, gloves, rings) [to]	끼다
wear headgear [to]	쓰다
weather	날씨
weather forecast	일기예보
wedding	결혼식
wedding gown	웨딩드레스
wedding hall	결혼식장
wedding hall	예식장
Wednesday	수요일
week	주
weekend	주말
weight	무게
well	잘
well; It's hard to say	글쎄요
west	서
Western medicine	서양의학
Western style	서양식
Western-style (food)	양식
what	뭐
	무엇
what date	며칠
what matter	웬일
what place, where	어디
what, what kind of	무슨
when	언제
which	어느
which, what kind of	어떤
white	흰색
who	누구
who	누가 (누구+가)
whole world [the]	전세계
why	왜
wife	아내
win [to]	이기다
wind	바람
window seat	창가 좌석
winter	겨울
wish	소원
wish [to]	기원하다
	원하다
with	하고
with a flash	깜빡
withdraw (money) [to]	찾다
without doing anything further	그만
woman	여자
won (Korean currency)	원 (₩)
work	일
work [to]	일하다
workplace	직장
World Cup	월드컵
worry	고민(하다)
worry [to]	걱정하다
worry, concern	걱정
worth	짜리
worth, value	어치
Wow!	와
wrap [to]	싸다
write [to]	쓰다
write down [to]	적다
writer	작가
written (exam)	필기 (시험)
yard	마당
	정원
yeah	응*plain*
year (counter)	년
years old	살
yellow	노란색
yes, I see, okay	네/예
yesterday	어제
yet, still	아직
	아직도

you	너*plain*	youngest child	막내
younger brother	남동생	Youngseo region	영서
younger sibling	동생	yut game	윷놀이
younger sister	여동생	zoo	동물원